Contents

Section 3　Special Occasions

Notes on using the book

These outlines are written so that the whole class will be involved in a variety of ways: singing, drama, painting, acting, drawing and so on. They are offered as suggestions and teachers should feel free to select and adapt material to suit their own situation. The children may well come up with suggestions for music or rewrite the drama in their own words for example. They cover a wide range of content, style and complexity in the hope that there is something both for the older and younger classes. They will need some practice but hopefully this will not take too much time.

Hymns and songs have not been suggested as each school has its own repertoire. As an alternative class assembly you might like to ask your children to choose some of their favourite songs to sing and then explain why they have chosen them, like a version of the TV programme *Songs of Praise*.

Ideas for prayers have generally not been included either, leaving it up to the teacher to decide what is suitable for the school. It also gives freedom for those children who want to write their own prayers.

Most of the outlines include a Bible base section which is intended as background reading for the teacher and not necessarily for the children. It is suggested that the Good News or New International children's version of the Bible is used in any work you do with the children and it is these versions that have been quoted in this book.

There are suggestions for preparation work in the class to use with children taking the assembly and also follow-up work which could be used in the other classes too, so that the assembly will not be seen totally in isolation. There is a resources section at the end of the book to help with class work.

I encourage you to read the opening chapter by Trevor Cooling. He makes some important observations about our handling of assemblies, particularly those involving class participation.

Starting Points: the characteristics of assemblies

I have a recurring nightmare. It goes back to my previous life some years past, when I was in charge of the assembly programme at my school. One of my responsibilities was to organise twice yearly acts of worship for the whole school to celebrate the festivals of Christmas and Easter. After six years of carrying that responsibility I felt I had given as much as I could – my creative energies had been drained away. My nightmare is that I am again required to generate yet more innovative ideas which will make these events a worthwhile and positive experience for pupils and staff alike, and that irrespective of their sympathy or animosity for things Christian! I know from many conversations that there are not a few primary school teachers who share my nightmare when their turn to organise the class assembly comes round. In the midst of all the demands of the classroom today, the class assembly can be the last straw.

Of course one of the characteristics of nightmares is that situations often appear worse in the middle of the night than when viewed from the perspective of daylight. One of the things that used to help enormously in putting my particular nightmare into perspective was when someone (usually my wife!) came up with the brilliant idea which seemed to break the log jam and release my own creativity and enthusiasm. At the end of struggling with all the difficulties and demands of mounting such events, the final result was usually something that was well worth doing and appreciated by most people present. It is one of those strange features of assemblies that many teachers find them at one and the same time both the most demanding and the most rewarding responsibility that they have to fulfil.

The purpose of this book is to provide busy teachers with a range of ideas for class assembly. It is essentially designed to turn nightmares into pleasant dreams! In preparing the outlines we have sought to fulfil the legal requirements as laid down in the 1988 Education Act for England and Wales, the Education (Scotland) Act of 1980 and the legislation of 1947 which still governs assemblies in Northern Ireland. Particular attention has been paid to the interpretations of these given by the English Department for Education (formerly the DES, now known by its new initials DFE) in various letters and in Circular 3/89 and by the Scottish HMI Report of 1989. We have also taken careful account of the developing consensus amongst teachers as to the aims and purposes of an assembly.

Assembly or Worship?
An important preliminary consideration concerns terminology. We are using the word assembly because that is the word most familiar to teachers to describe the type of event this book deals with. It also sounds a lot more friendly than 'collective worship' or 'religious observance'. However, in terms of the legislation the correct terms are in fact 'collective worship' for England, Wales and Northern Ireland and 'religious observance' for Scotland.

In trying to clarify the distinction the DFE in England has provided some helpful guidance. This emphasises four things as characteristic of school worship:
a) It should reflect something special or separate from ordinary school activities.
b) It should be concerned with reverence or veneration paid to a being or power regarded as supernatural or divine.
c) Pupils should be able to perceive these two features.
d) Seemingly everyday activities can be included as long as they are appropriate to the act of worship as a whole.

Strictly understood, an assembly is an administrative event which may include reference to social and moral issues, but does not incorporate these characteristics of school worship. The distinctive point about worship is that it is an experiential exploration of religious belief and not a purely secular event. So it is important to remember that, although we use the popular term assembly, the purpose of this book is to resource collective worship and religious observance, as defined by the law.

The Characteristics of Assembly

There are four key characteristics of school assembly which have been at the forefront of our minds in preparing this collection.

Christian

All the assemblies in this book are wholly Christian in the sense that they do not draw specifically on the teachings of other religions. They are not denominational, but rather focus on those broad traditions of belief which are shared by Christians generally. Each assembly is based on particular Bible passages.

They are also not narrowly Christian in the sense that they are of no relevance or interest to children who do not have a Christian background. Many of the assemblies focus on issues and values which are part of shared human experience and of concern to many belief systems, for example the importance of concern for those less fortunate than ourselves. The aim is to draw on Christian teachings as a way of encouraging children to reflect on their own attitudes, values and actions and thereby promote their spiritual development.

These assemblies are therefore in accordance with the advice given by the DFE in England which requires that broadly Christian worship:
a) must contain an element related specifically to the traditions of Christian belief
b) must accord some special status to Jesus Christ
c) must not be distinctive of any particular denomination
d) may contain elements common to Christianity and other religions.

9

Collective

A distinction that has been given considerable prominence is that made between corporate and collective worship. Basically corporate worship is what happens when a like-minded group of people meet together to worship God. In most schools that cannot be assumed to be happening because children and staff represent a wide variety of religious commitments and none.

Collective worship, on the other hand, is an activity which is designed to draw together people of many different commitments in a shared educational experience. It is unlike anything that goes on within churches and is not the same as worship as traditionally practised by Christians. Educational collective worship is an occasion for gaining insights into, and reflecting on, Christian beliefs and not usually, as is the case within the faith community, for giving adoration to God as the focus of faith.

The defining characteristic of collective worship is then that it is an opportunity for children and staff together to learn something **about** and even something **from** Christianity in a way that is appropriate for each individual. For some people, and this will vary greatly from school to school, collective worship will also be an opportunity to learn and worship specifically **as** a Christian. But this should never be presumed.

Compulsory

One of the oddest things about school worship is that it is compulsory. Children have to attend unless they are specifically withdrawn by their parents, and very few children are. It is of course in one sense a complete nonsense to say that worship can be compulsory, just as it is a complete nonsense to make being in love compulsory. Properly understood, worship has to be a voluntary response. What is in fact compulsory is that pupils attend.

However the legislation implies that schools should aim for more than reducing their assembly truancy rate. This is borne out by subsequent advice. Thus HMI in Scotland, in their report on Religious Observance, write that 'active participation is essential

10

to the quality of the experience'. In England the DFE has stated that attendance should be more than 'simply passive'. The aim is not just to ensure that disgruntled observers actually take their seats in the school hall. However, if active participation is to be achieved in a way that puts all children and staff at their ease, it is clear that methods have to be developed which respect the integrity of people with very different faith commitments.

One important way of achieving this 'participation with integrity' is to ensure that children and staff are free to respond in a way that is appropriate for them. This will mean carefully considering how the family background of each of the children can be respected. Each child, depending on his or her personal circumstances, will need to be free either to identify or not to identify with any particular act of worship. This means that responses at a number of levels must all be affirmed. So, for example, for one child an appropriate response may simply be to reflect on the importance of a particular belief for Christians whereas another child may actively embrace that belief in a response of personal commitment. What is quite clear is that any attempt to pressurise pupils to assent to particular beliefs, or even to make them feel implicitly that to assent is the 'done thing', is inadmissible in the school situation. Such behaviour is an abuse of a captive audience.

The most important means of ensuring this protection of other people's integrity lie in the attitudes and language of the teacher responsible for the assembly. We all know what it is like to have someone trying to impose their beliefs on us. We feel cornered and it is not a pleasant experience. However we are all aware of how different it is when someone seeks to share an idea that is precious to them with us. It is rather like entering into someone's enthusiasm for their 'holiday of a lifetime' photographs! It is the latter feeling that we as teachers should be trying to create. Achieving that is very much a direct consequence of our own attitudes. We convey these through our language, which should never actively seek or presume assent on the part of colleagues or children. So for example, prayer should always be introduced by a phrase like:

'I am now going to say a prayer. I want you all to listen carefully. If you like you can close your eyes to help you concentrate. When I finish I will say "Amen". If you want to you can also say "Amen" which means that you agree with my prayer.'

This 'non-presumptive' language is very important to the success of collective worship. Dogmatism should be shunned.

It is also important that children are not asked to do anything explicitly Christian if this would be inappropriate to their family background. Examples might be singing hymns which entail worship of Jesus, participation in a Eucharist or involving Muslim children in drama about Jesus. It is the teacher's responsibility to make careful judgements as to what may or may not be appropriate for particular children.

Celebration

All this may make collective worship seem fraught with problems and better avoided. That is not an impression I wish to create. I therefore intend to end on a positive note.

Perhaps one of the most important features of collective worship is that it should be a celebration. The fact that class assembly is a co-operative activity between a number of children gives a much greater opportunity for celebration than is the case with the 'one man band' model where a teacher leads what often amounts to a 'moral thought for the day'. Class assembly is essentially a celebration of the learning that children have been engaged in during their work together. As an educational exercise it constitutes a presentation by the children of the enquiry that has been conducted within their class. It becomes Christian collective worship when the focus of the celebration is their class exploration of certain Christian beliefs and of the reverence paid by Christians to God and Jesus.

As a celebration of learning, assembly should draw on a variety of participatory methods, including drama, music, dance, display etc. It provides Christian teachers and children with an opportunity to celebrate their faith and to share it with others. As long as this is done in ways appropriate for school, and this chapter has pointed those out, class assembly can be a most positive experience and provide children with a memory of a real 'occasion'. We hope that the assembly suggestions which follow will be catalysts for such occasions.

Trevor Cooling
Projects Officer at Stapleford House, the training centre of the Association of Christian Teachers.
October 1992

1 All about us

1 Fruit parade

Aim

To show that what is on the *inside* counts – not what people look like on the outside.

Bible base

1 Samuel 16:1–13. David is chosen king of Israel.

Preparation

Bring in a banana, orange, apple and dirty potato and ask the group to vote for the most attractive object. The 'spud' usually comes bottom of the poll as it is the least attractive. Make the point that although we are put off by the dirty appearance of the potato, inside it may be in much better condition.

Wrap some sweets in brown paper and some stones in colourful wrapping paper and see which they choose.

Swap the labels on a number of cans. Ask the children to guess what's inside, then surprise them!

Give the children a number of qualities, eg kindness, sense of humour including good-looking, and ask them which are important when they choose a friend.

Show the children a number of pictures of people and ask them whom they like the look of and why.

15

Look at the story of the choosing of David to be king (1 Samuel 16:1–13) showing that God looks not at the outward appearance but at the heart.

Do some fruit tasting.

Draw the outsides and insides of various fruits.

Prepare fruit costumes and boards showing fruit cut in half.

Presentation

Participants: Compere, judges, fruits, the rest of the class can be the audience.

Leader: We'd like to welcome you to our Fruit Parade. Let me hand over to our compere for the occasion . . .

Compere: May I introduce you to our judges? Here we have Jason Donovan, Jeff Banks from the Clothes Show and our special guest, Princess Diana. Thank you for coming along to be our judges. Now let's meet our contestants.

(*As fruit parade onto the catwalk dressed in appropriate colours the compere, in bow tie, says a few words.*)

Compere: Here we have Adam Apple from France. Doesn't he look amazing? Adam occasionally gives people the pip, although he's very sweet most of the time.

Next on the catwalk we have Belinda Banana all the way from Jamaica. Belinda says that if her father knew she had entered he'd skin her alive!

Percy Pear comes from Kent. He's looking very cool in a nice dark green number.

Prunella Peach has jetted over from Spain to be with us. She hopes one day to take over the family business, peaches and cream.

Lucy Lemon normally lives in Israel. She's known as 'Juicy Lucy' to her friends.

Let's have a huge round of applause for our stunning contestants. Thank you!

Now while the judges make their decision let's hear . . . (*at this point a group of children would sing, or play their recorders etc.*)

Compere (*after consulting the judges*): I'm afraid the judges can't make up their minds. They want to taste the competitors!

(The fruits parade again with boards showing their fruit cut in half, with maggots etc.)

Compere: Oh dear, Adam seems to have a rather large maggot eating its way through him. I'm afraid he can't win.

Belinda is all black and rotten inside – what a disappointment!

Percy has gone all soft and mushy underneath that skin of his. I don't suppose he has much chance now.

What's this inside Prunella? I do believe it's a heart of stone! She can't win either.

Our last winner must be Lucy, she surely must be the winner . . . but no . . . she is completely bitter inside.

What a disaster – we shall have to abandon this competition!

Leader: It's what's inside that counts, not what people look like on the outside. When God looks at us he looks at us on the inside. This is what the Bible says: 'God does not see the same way people see. People look on the outside of a person, but the Lord looks at the heart.' (1 Samuel 16:7(b))

Follow up

Read 'It's Not Much Fun Being a Slug' from *Ignatius Goes Fishing* by Philip Welsh, published by Scripture Union.

2 What am I worth?

Aim

To show that we are all valuable in the eyes of God.

Bible base

Matthew 6:25–30. God's care for us.

Preparation

Bring in various objects worth different amounts and get the children to guess what their price is, based on the TV programme *The Price is Right*. Include some things which may not be very expensive but are rare, hand made or have sentimental value. Talk about whether cost and value are the same thing. Ask the children what things are valuable to them. Find out what people are made up of (chemicals and water). Is that all there is to us? Discuss what other qualities make a person special.

Have a balloon debate, where different people argue their case for not being thrown out of a balloon. Talk about how we value people. Is it by what they do or what they are?

Pass round a 'magic box' with a mirror inside it. Explain to the children there is something very special inside it. Tell them to have a look, but don't tell anyone.

Discuss with the children the worth of a prominent member of school eg the head. Imagine s/he had been kidnapped. Encourage them to think of reasons why they would pay the ransom.

Presentation

Leader: Today we're going to think about things that are valuable. Can anyone give an example of something they think is worth a lot?

Here the children could show things they regard as valuable and explain why.

Leader: We have been looking at what we're made of and how much we are worth.

Reader: A person is nothing but . . .

Fat enough for seven bars of soap

Iron enough for one nail

Sugar enough for seven cups of tea

Phosphorus enough to tip 2,200 matches

Magnesium enough for one dose of salts

Sulphur enough to rid one dog of fleas

Water enough to fill six buckets

Leader: (*Put up the list of chemicals and ask the children to guess how much they would cost. The price comes to under £10*). So really we're not worth much, are we?

(At this stage a group of children could come in and kidnap the head or some other member of the school. The choice should be made carefully, and the victim should be primed! They leave a ransom note explaining that they want money if s/he is to be returned.)

Other members of the class come forward with monopoly money and say what they would pay and why! This could be humorous. Eventually enough money is raised and the victim is returned.

Leader: The things that are in our bodies may not be worth very much, but as people we are very valuable. Sometimes we might not feel very valuable, but listen to what Jesus said in the Bible about how much we are worth.

Reader: Jesus said, 'If God cares about all the birds in the sky, how much more does he care about people? If God can make the flowers beautiful, how much more does he look after humans?'

Leader: The Bible also says that God values us so highly that he was willing to give up the life of his son for us, as a sort of ransom, so that we could be friends with him. Just as you look after a valuable object very carefully, so people should be cared for and loved.

Follow up

Do some work to show that each of us is unique.

Each child brings in a photo of themselves, sticks the photo on a piece of paper and then writes around the photo under the headings 'My special people', 'My special places', 'What I'm good at'.

Use 'Bags of confidence'. Each child has a paper bag with their name on it. The bags are passed round and the others write on a slip of paper what they like about that person and put it into the bag.

Make their own coat of arms.

Read to the class 'Napoleon the Envious Earwig' from a book called *Ignatius Goes Fishing* by Philip Welsh, published by Scripture Union.

3   What can I do?

Aim

To show the children that we all have gifts and that we should use them to the best of our ability to serve God and others.

Bible base

Luke 19:11–26. The parable of the gold coins.

Preparation

Give each child a piece of paper and ask them to write down the thing they think they are best at. It can be anything, not just a school subject, but something they do at home or a characteristic. Then ask them to write something they would like to be good at. Tell them not to let anyone else see their paper. The children choose a partner and ask them to write down what they think they are best at. When they have all done this let them compare what they have written with what their friends think. Ask if they think the thing they would like to be able to do is better or more important than the thing they can do.

Discuss this and help the children to see that we all have different gifts that are equally important, and it's the way we use them that counts. Read or tell the story of the gold coins (or the talents in Matthew 25:14–30) and explain that the man who had one talent was not punished because he had only one but because he did not use it.

Presentation

Leader: We all have different things that we are good at, whether it is singing, playing football, or helping at home. Here are some of the things we can do.

eg **Child 1:** I have painted a picture (*shows picture*)

Child 2: I have written a poem (*reads poem*)

Child 3: I have made a model (*shows model*)

Child 4: I have done some maths (*shows book*)

Child 5: I have learned a new tune (*plays/sings*)

Child 6: These are gifts (*several children could bring out a banner showing pictures of wrapped presents.*)

Leader: God has given us all different gifts, and he wants us to use them and to help other people. Jesus told a story about three people who were given gifts. Listen to how they used them.

Reader 1: There was once a man . . . Luke 19:12–14

Reader 2: Luke 19:15–19

Reader 3: Luke 19:20–23

Reader 4: Luke 19:24–26

Leader: Our class are now going to show a modern version of the parable.

Narrator: There was once a man who sold brushes. He had a number of door-to-door sellers working for him. One day, he called some of them to him.

Boss: I'm going on a long trip to find out about brushes used in other countries. While I am gone, I'm leaving you to look after the business here. I'll give each of you a suitcase full of brushes, dusters and polishes. See what you can do with them while I'm gone.

Narrator: There are a lot of countries in the world and in each of those countries there are a lot of brushes. The man was gone for a long time. When he returned he called the brush-sellers to him.

Boss: Tell me what you have done with your brushes, number one?

Number one: I sold all the brushes, dusters and polishes that you gave me. With the money I was able to buy another two cases of brushes. When I sold all these, I was able to buy some more, and so on. Now I have ten people working for me.

Boss: I am very pleased with you. I will put you in charge of my brush-selling business in ten different countries. Number two?

Number two: I also sold everything and bought more. I now have five people working for me.

Boss: Well done! I will put you in charge of five different countries. What about you, number three?

Number three: Well sir, I have the suitcase you gave me here. I have kept it hidden under my bed. Knowing that you are a hard man to work for, I hid the case away because I was afraid I might lose or damage it. I did not want to make you angry.

Boss: You have made me very angry! Even if you had just sold all the brushes to (a hardware shop) I would have had *something* in return. Those brushes are all old-fashioned now! How can you call yourself a brush-seller? Give your brushes to number one and get out of my sight!

Reader 5: Jesus said these words, 'You are like light for the world. No-one lights a lamp and puts it under a bowl; instead he puts it on a lampstand where it gives light to everyone in the house. In the same way your light must shine before people, so that they will see the good things you do and praise your father in heaven'.

Leader: The Bible says that all the things that we can do well are the gifts God has given us. Everyone has a gift. Think about how you can use *your* gift to make other people happy.

Follow up

Give the children the opportunity of choosing a piece of work they'd really like to do, eg. artwork, lettering, writing stories. Encourage them to keep it up until they have produced the very best of which they are capable. Make a display.

In pairs talk about things they can do. Write them down on an 'I can' leaf and stick it onto an 'I can' tree.

Read the stories 'Superfrog' and 'The Revenge of Jasper the Toad' from *Ignatius Goes Fishing* by Philip Welsh, published by Scripture Union.

The children could interview teachers about their hobbies and interests.

4   The body

Aim

To show that we are all important to each other.

Bible base

1 Corinthians 12:14–27. One body with many parts.

Preparation

This assembly could be incorporated into a topic on the body.
Play a co-operation game. The following is an example. Divide
the class into five smaller groups which each represent a body
part eg eyes, ears, hands, feet, mouth. The five groups must
all work together to rescue 'life' before it dies. 'Life' is symbol-
ised by a kitchen timer that is set for thirty minutes and
locked in a box. When the timer goes off 'life' is dead. The only
way 'life' can be saved is for the groups, working together, to
complete the tasks that lead to the key which opens the box
and lets 'life' out.

In order to do the tasks, each group functions mostly as it
would in a normal body ie. an eye cannot hear and an ear
cannot see. Therefore everyone except the eyes must be blindfolded.

When the game begins the task is written and presented
to the eyes, who whisper it to the ears, who then whisper it
to the mouths, who can then verbalise it to the rest of the
body. Whenever the group go anywhere, the feet must carry
the eyes and the remaining members of the body must follow
behind in single file, holding onto each others' waists. The

eyes in that case are allowed to speak, giving instructions to the rest of the body.

The tasks may be fairly simple; three or four are enough. For example, the hands should feed a biscuit to the mouths while being guided by the eyes. Feet should then carry the ears to a place, followed by the rest of the body.

The last task leads to the envelope that contains the key to the box. The hands must use the key to open it, guided by the eyes, carried by the feet.

Talk about the game and how each part of the body did or did not function.

Give groups of children words that they spell out, using their bodies to make the letters, the others guessing what the word is.

Look at Paul's analogy of the body in 1 Corinthians 12:14–27. Prepare four pictures of large lips, eyes, a foot and an ear.

Presentation

As an introduction the class are in a line passing bags (or equivalent) along from one end to the other. Each child should have a different action eg. passing overhead, side to side but they all fit together. After a while one or two drop out and because their action is needed the line disintegrates.

Narrator: In that line everyone was needed because they had a job to do. As soon as someone gave up things did not work so well. Today we want to think about something where all the parts work together. Can you guess what it is?

(*Here a group of children could spell 'THE BODY' using their bodies to spell the words.*)

Our class have been looking at the different parts of the body.

(*Some children could share some of the work they've done on the body.*)

We've discovered that all the parts have different functions and work together. Let's show you. I've told (N) there is a sweet on the table. He looks and walks over to it, picks it up and eats it. Let's try that again but this time if (N) had an eye instead of an ear (*attach one of the large eyes to his ear*) he wouldn't hear me. If he had an eye instead of a leg (*attach eye to leg*) he couldn't walk over. If he had an eye instead of a hand (*eye stuck on hand*) he couldn't pick it up, if he had an eye instead of a mouth (*eye on mouth*) he couldn't eat it. The same applies to (N). She can walk over and pick the sweet up and eat it (*she does so*). But what if she had lips instead of eyes, legs, hands, ears? (*Each time lips are attached to the body part mentioned.*)

We need each part of our body, yet each part is different. Listen to what the Bible says.

Reader: A person's body has more than one part. It has many parts. The foot might say . . .

Child holding large foot: I am not a hand, so I am not part of the body.

Reader: But saying this would not stop the foot from being part of the body. The ear might say . . .

Ear: I am not an eye, so I am not part of the body.

Reader: But saying this would not make the ear stop being part of the body. If the whole body were an eye, the body would not be able to hear. If the whole body were an ear, the body would not be able to smell anything. If each part of the body were the same part, there would be no body. But God put the parts in the body as he wanted them. He made a place for each of them.

Narrator: Different people are a bit like the parts of a body. Each part is different. The eye isn't useless because it can't run or the nose because it can't write. God made us all different. Each person has her or his own gifts which s/he can use to help others. We all need each other.

Follow up

Do some work on showing that each of us is unique. (See assemblies **What am I worth?** and **What can I do?** for further suggestions.

Draw 'body people' ie. draw a foot with hands, eyes and a mouth.

5 Hands

Aim

To look at how we use our hands and to show how Jesus used his hands.

Bible base

Mark 5: 25–34 and Luke 5:12–16. Jesus healing the sick.

Preparation

Make shapes with hands, eg shadow pictures.

Make different noises with hands.

Prepare a number of activities using hands that the children could demonstrate in assembly, eg playing an instrument, painting, modelling clay, origami, putting on a coat, a handstand.

Talk about how you can use your hands to help or to be unkind.

Look at fingerprints through a magnifying glass. Try to copy them.

Look at some braille. Find out how the sense of touch works.

Play a blindfold game where the children have to guess the objects through touch.

Ask the children to imagine what the worst thing they could touch would be. Look at the story of Jesus healing the man with leprosy (Luke 5) and explain that people thought touching a person with leprosy was revolting. Find out about leprosy.

Also look at the story of the woman touching Jesus (Mark

5). The children could make up their own news reports on the stories or use the ones below for the assembly.

Presentation

Introduction: We use our hands in many different ways. Here different children demonstrate various ways of using hands or talk about things they've discovered to do with hands, touch etc.

Play a blindfold game where some volunteers from the rest of the school have to guess what the objects are.

Narrator (*pretending to be in TV studio*): The Bible has a number of reports where Jesus touched people and they were healed. We're going to interview a couple of people who were alive at the time of Jesus. These two people have something in common. They both experienced the power of Jesus' touch in their lives but in different ways. Let's go over to our news reporter in Galilee.

Simon: Hello this is Simon from the Galilee Gazette and I have with me Hannah from a local village. Let me ask her a few questions. How long had you been ill when you met Jesus?

H: I had been ill for twelve years.

S: What was wrong with you?

H: I had an illness which meant I could not stop bleeding inside.

S: Couldn't you get a doctor to treat you?

H: Yes. I was treated by many doctors but none of them could make me better. I spent all the money I could on doctors.

S: What made you ask Jesus for help?

H: I'd heard a great deal about Jesus, how he could help people and how many had been healed. I was too shy and too scared to ask for help but I worked out that if I could touch the hem of his cloak I would be healed and he would never know. So that's what I did.

S: But he did find out, didn't he?

H: Yes. I don't know how. It was very crowded but he seemed to know someone had touched him. He asked who it was.

S: What happened then?

H: I had to own up. I knelt at his feet and then he said something wonderful. He said 'Go in peace. Your faith has made you well'.

S: And you were well after that?

H: Oh yes. I was so happy. I'll never forget that day.

S: Thank you, Hannah. Back to the studio.

Narrator: Thank you, Simon. We've had another extraordinary report from the Nazareth News. Let's go over to our reporter Mary to find out the latest.

M: Thank you. I have Benjamin here and he has quite a story to tell.

B: I used to have a disease called leprosy.

M: What's that like?

B: Well, it's a disease that affects the nerve endings of the skin. I had horrible patches on my face and body. Of course my family threw me out, as everyone thought that leprosy was very catching and they didn't want to get it themselves.

M: So what did you do?

B: Well, I had heard of Jesus and all the things he was said to have done. I knew he could make me better but I was afraid he wouldn't want to come near me. No-one else did.

M: So what happened next?

B: Well, when I heard that Jesus was in our village I waited until everyone was listening to Jesus. I rushed up to him and pleaded with him to make me better. I knew he could if he wanted to.

M: I expect Jesus was a bit surprised, wasn't he?

B: I don't know, but do you know what he did next? He actually touched me. No-one had touched me for years and then he said, "I do want to heal you. Be healed." Just like that.

M: Were the people surprised?

B: Surprised? They were horrified that Jesus would dare to touch someone with leprosy.

M: Were you healed?

B: Yes. All my leprosy went from that moment.

M: What did you do next?

B: Jesus told me to go and report to the priest to prove that I was well. Then I went home to my family again. I will never forget the way Jesus touched me that day.

M: Thank you very much, Benjamin. Back to the studio.

Narrator: Two remarkable stories about Jesus, and how he used his hands to make people well and happy.

Follow up

Look up other Bible stories where hands were used to help eg. Matthew 8:14,15 (healing of Peter's mother-in-law), John 12:1–8 (Mary annoints Jesus' feet) John 13:3–12 (Jesus washes disciples' feet) Mark 10:13–16 (children in his arms).

Use hands for measuring.

The following mime could also be used in assembly on hands, although it may not be appropriate in some situations.

God gave us hands. (*Two people face the audience. They point upwards and then show their hands*).

Hands that build . . . (*they each build something*)

Or hands that destroy . . . (*one destroys what the other built*)

Hands that love . . . (*they hug each other*)

Or hands that hate . . . (*they push each other away*)

Hands that help . . . (*one helps the other to lift a heavy load*)

Or hands that are lazy . . . (*one of them lets go of the load and the other falls over*)

Hands that give . . . (*one of them gives something*)

Or hands that grab . . . (*they both try to grab something*)

Hands that greet . . . (*they shake hands*)

Or hands that are afraid . . . (*they avoid each other and fold their arms*)

Hands that are open . . . (*they face each other and extend open hands to one another*)

Or hands that hide things . . . (*they turn and hide from each other*)

Hands that are satisfied . . . (*they rub tummies*)

Or hands that are greedy . . . (*they try to get more*)

God held out his hands to us by sending Jesus . . . (*they face each other, one holds out his hand and the other looks at him*)

So that we could be friends with him again . . . (*they hug each other*)

People nailed Jesus' hands to the cross . . . (*one of them takes the other by the hands and nails him to an imaginary cross*)

He died that people may be friends with God again . . . (*the one on the cross dies*)

(Taken from *Shipmates*, copyright SU Missions Department 1989.)

6   The hole

Aim

To show that Jesus can be with us and help us with our difficulties.

Bible base

Matthew 28:20. Jesus' commission to the disciples.

Preparation

Brainstorm or prepare a word box or web of 'people who help me'.

In pairs children think about a typical day at home or school where they might need help.

Presentation

Narrator: Once upon a time there was a window cleaner. One day when he was busy cleaning his windows, a strong gust of wind came along and blew him off his ladder. Luckily for him, he happened to land in a hole that had been dug by workmen just the day before. Unluckily for him, he couldn't get out of the hole. As time went by several people came along.

(*As each person introduces themselves the window cleaner asks them to help him out of the hole.*)

1. I am a news reporter. As always, I'm first on the scene of any major newsworthy incident. Now sir, can you give me a few details of what happened? Where did you fall from?

What made you fall? Which window were you cleaning at the time? What time was it when you fell?

2. I'm a photographer for the local paper. I want to get a really good picture of what happened. Could you just hold still please, sir? Lovely! Now, perhaps one from another angle? Er, I don't suppose you could smile, sir, could you? That's perfect! Thank you very much sir. Should be in today's edition.

3. I am a tax man. I work for the local council. Tell me, sir, have you been living in this hole long? Is anyone living in there with you? Are you planning on living there much longer? You see, sir, I'm probably going to have to ask you to pay taxes on this hole, sir. I'll just go and get you a copy of form E/103/CW/289 to fill in. Back in a minute, sir.

4. I'm a council inspector. Excuse me sir, but have you got planning permission for this hole? If you haven't, I'm afraid I shall have to ask you to fill it in. I mean, we can't have people going around digging holes all over the place can we?

5. I'm a geologist. I study rock formations and how the earth is made up. This looks like a particularly interesting hole, sir. Just look at those rock formations! Well, well, well . . . I hope you realise how lucky you are to have landed in such an interesting hole, sir.

6. I'm a scientist. I have a very logical brain and can usually work out the answer to most problems. Now let me see, sir. What will it take to extract you from this hole? I'll just go away and work out the formula needed.

7. I'm an optimist. I always look on the bright side of life. Just think, sir, you could have fallen into a hole full of water and drowned by now. How lucky you are! Isn't life wonderful! 'Oh what a beautiful morning! Oh what a beautiful day! I've got a wonderful feeling that this must be your lucky day!'

8. I'm a pessimist. I always see the worst in a situation. Oh dear, oh dear, sir. You're in a real fix, aren't you? Oh dearie me. In fact things are really at their worst, aren't they? Oh dear.

9. I'm a self-pitying person. I always think I'm worse off than anyone else. You think you've got problems sir! Huh! You should have seen the last hole I fell into. Deep? Makes this one look like a puddle! And no one even spoke to me, let alone tried to help me out of it. Believe me you're lucky, very lucky!

10. Hello, I'm an evasive person. I try to avoid talking about other people's problems. Hello there! Nice day, isn't it? Did you see the golf on Saturday? What about Nick Faldo and that hole in . . . (Oh no, mustn't mention holes) . . . er . . . fancy a polo, you know that mint with a (Oh dear, don't mention holes!) . . . no, have a piece of chocolate instead. Tell you what, have the *whole* bar . . . oh dear . . . oh well, bye for now!

11. I am a school teacher. I've told you three times to be careful on that ladder! When will you learn? You're not setting a very good example to these younger children you know! I suggest you fill this hole in for homework.

12. I'm a policeman. Hello, hello, hello. What have we got here then? I shall have to arrest you, sir, if you continue to loiter here. Now move along, there's a good chap.

13. Hello, I'm Jesus. Give me your hand and I'll help you get out of that hole.

Man: Thank you very much. Bye!

(*Jesus follows man*)

Man: What are you doing?

Jesus: I'm following you. I'm coming with you. You'll probably find you'll need me again sooner or later.

Leader: As you have just seen, we often get ourselves into tricky situations and we sometimes struggle to get out of them by ourselves. Christians know that by having Jesus as a friend doesn't stop you from getting into difficulties, but it certainly helps when you want to get out of them.

7 An old man and his camels

Aim

To show that we need help from the outside and that God can provide that help.

(*This is on a similar theme to the previous assembly outline and the same introductory activities could be used.*)

Presentation

Narrator: Once upon a time there was an old man. He knew that he was going to die soon so he called his three sons to him to give them his final wishes. To the eldest son he gave one half of all he owned. (*He gives his son a card with 1/2 written on it*). To the second son he gave a third. (*He gives him a card with 1/3 written on it*). To the youngest son he gave a ninth (*He too gets a card with 1/9 written on it*). He blessed them and died.

When the sons set about sharing his possessions, they found it impossible. Their father had left them seventeen camels. (*Other children can be these camels, they could wear masks or draw pictures of camels which they carry*).

How could they divide seventeen by two, three, or nine? (*They each try to do this, it can't be done. They can make it funny by deciding whether to chop someone in half long ways or straight across the middle etc.*)

Hearing of their trouble, an old friend of their father's came and said:

Friend: I have but one camel, but I shall give it to you and you will have eighteen to divide among you.

Narrator: The eldest son took his half of the eighteen

which is nine (*act this out*).

The second son took his third which is six (*act this out*).

The third son took his ninth, which is two (*act this out*).

Then they saw that their old friend's camel still remained, for indeed 9+6+2=17. Full of joy, each took his own camels and went home.

The story shows us that we all need help from the outside, help from other people from time to time. The Bible is full of stories of how God helps his people.

(Some children could read prayers they've written, asking for God's help in various situations in the world, for people who are sick etc.)

Follow up

Discuss how God can help today.

Look at stories from the Bible showing how people are strengthened by God to overcome obstacles and do important work (eg David, Gideon). Look at some modern examples eg Mother Teresa.

8   All about a water pump

Aim

To show that God knows all about us because he made us.

Bible base

Psalm 139: 1–6, 13–18. God's knowledge and care of us.

Preparation

Play a game where the children write down several state-
ments about themselves; three are facts, one is fiction. They
try and guess which is the false one for the others.

Make shields or fact-files about themselves.

Talk about the people who know them best.

Look at the story about the water pump. Ask them who
they think is the best person to help them.

Presentation

Narrator: Our story is about a village which had a water
pump.

*(One child acts as the water pump, one arm as handle, the
other as a spout, and another child can be the bucket.).*

Each day the villagers would come and get their water
from the pump.

*(Various children make their way to the pump and collect
water, having a chat as they go).*

Everything was fine until one day, disaster struck! The
water pump didn't work! It was crucial to do something

quickly as the whole village depended on the water pump for their water. The villagers got together to decide what should be done.

(*The class acting as villagers have a discussion among themselves*).

The policeman, Mr. Plod, stepped forward.

Mr. Plod: I know what to do. (*He talks sternly to the water pump*) I command you to work in the name of the law. Otherwise I will have no option but to arrest you!

Narrator: A villager came forward to try the pump. He pumped and pumped . . . but no water came out. An old man was watching what was going on. He spoke up . . .

Old man: You know the problem is on the inside.

Narrator: But no-one took any notice of him. A small girl on her way to school piped up . . .

Small girl: I know how to fix it!

Narrator: She ran forward and gave the pump an almighty kick. She then tried pumping the handle but of course no water came out. Meanwhile the old man was still watching . . .

Old man: You know, the problem is on the inside.

Narrator: But no-one listened. The mayoress decided to come and take a look herself.

Mayoress: Well, look how shabby this water pump is! No wonder it won't work. What it needs is a good lick of paint. I think pink with blue spots would be nice.

Narrator: Mr Dulux the painter was called to the scene. He duly gave the pump a brand new coat of paint.

Mr Dulux: There you are madam, that should do it. It's quick drying paint so you can try again.

Narrator: One of the villagers eagerly stepped forward. She pumped and pumped . . . but no water came out. What were they going to do? The old man who had stuck around to see what would happen spoke again.

Old man: You know, the problem is on the inside.

Narrator: The mayoress called together another conference of all the villagers. (*Villagers have another discussion amongst themselves*)

They thought and thought. Who could they get to fix it? Eventually they called Mr Plug. Anyone guess what his job was? Yes, he used to be the plumber in the village. Mr Plug came along and took the lid off the top of the water pump and fiddled around inside. He put the top back on and stepped out of the way. Another villager tried the pump. He pumped and pumped and . . . water came out. The villagers were delighted and began cheering and celebrating.

(*Villagers shout and cheer*)

Narrator: How did Mr Plug know how to mend the water pump? Let's ask him . . .

Mr Plug: Well, you see I knew how the water pump worked because I was the one who made it. I put it together in the first place!

Leader: The Bible explains that the person who knows us best and understands how we work is God, because he made us. This is what the Bible says . . .

Reader: Psalm 139:1–4

Leader: Christians believe that God is the best person to help us when we have problems.

(*Some of the children could read their own prayers here if appropriate.*)

9 David and Goliath

Aim

To look at how we face difficult situations through the story of David and Goliath.

Bible base

1 Samuel 17. David defeats Goliath.

Preparation

Discuss with the children some things they can do and things they can't. What do they do about the things they can't do? Have they ever been asked to do something they thought was too difficult for them? How did they feel before and after doing it?

What difficult situations have they had to face? What did they do?

Brainstorm different situations they might find difficult eg joining a new club or trying something new and invent symbols for 'too dangerous', 'have a go but be careful' and 'OK go ahead'. After discussion the children draw the appropriate symbol for the situation (the risks will obviously be different for different children).

Look at the story of David and Goliath. What was the reaction of the Israelites to the problem? What did David do? How would he have been feeling?

The presentation of this assembly uses shadow puppets to tell the story. The children therefore need to draw outlines of the characters etc. Alternatively the children themselves make the shadows by standing behind the sheet. (Body movements should be exaggerated and slower than usual.)

To create the shadows you need a light source such as an overhead projector, a slide projector, or stage light. A screen can be either a blank white wall or a sheet stretched across the room. A sheet allows the shadows but not the players to be seen by the audience. The children will need to experiment in front of the light to find the best effects. Groups of children could be given different scenes to prepare eg Goliath challenging the Israelites, David going to Saul's camp, David visiting Saul, David defeating Goliath.

(This assembly is based on an idea from *Show Me* published by the Bible Society.)

Presentation

Leader: In our class we have been talking about things we can and can't do. Here are some of them.

Children show examples eg. multiplying 10x3 but not 6341x356!

We also talked about difficult situations we've had to face (*give examples if appropriate*).

Today we are going to show you a story about a time when the Israelites were facing a very difficult situation.

Scene 1: Goliath challenges the Israelites

Narrator 1: The Israelites were in a spot of bother.
Narrator 2: Their enemies, the Philistines had gathered an army to fight against Saul, who was king of Israel.
N1: Shepherds and farmers had left their homes to follow Saul. (*Shadows of soldiers*)
N2: The two armies faced each other across the valley; the Israelites on one hill, the Philistines on the other. (*Hills with valley in between*)
N1: Now the Philistines had fighting for them . . .
N2: A giant called Goliath.
(*Goliath appears*)
N1: He was three metres tall and had a voice to go with his size.

N2: His legs were like tree trunks.

N1: Every morning . . .

N2: Without fail . . .

N1: Goliath marched out and challenged the Israelites.

Goliath: Send out your champion to fight me. If I win, you surrender. If you win, we surrender! What's the matter, are you scared? (*Children could suggest what Goliath might say instead.*)

N2: He was so huge . . .

N1: And so well-armed no-one dared to fight him.

N2: The laughter of the Philistines could be heard echoing around the hills.

Scene 2: David at Saul's camp

N1: Now David was a shepherd boy, sent by his father to bring food for his brothers. (*David appears as a tiny shadow*)

N2: He might have been the youngest in the family but he was brave.

N1: He heard Goliath's challenge and asked who was going to fight.

N2: No-one moved.

N1: No-one stirred. They were too scared of what Goliath might do to them.

N2: David decided he would go.

David: After all, what's that heathen Philistine got against the armies of God?

N1: David's brothers were fed up with him and told him to go back to his sheep. This was a man's job.

Scene 3: David goes to Saul

N2: David didn't go home.

N1: He went to see Saul.

(*David kneels before Saul*)

David: I will fight the monster Goliath.

N2: Saul was unimpressed.

Saul: You! You're just a boy and he's been a soldier all his life.

David: So what! I'm a shepherd and I've been fighting bears and wolves all my life. God was with me then and looked after me. Anyway, Goliath looks like a bear.

42

N1: Saul was desperate so he agreed to let David try.

N2: Out came Saul's best armour . . . (*weapons added to David's shadow*)

N1: David tried to walk.

N2: He couldn't.

N1: He stumbled and fell.

N2: It took four men to lift him.

David: Take this lot off! I'm going to fight this my way.

N1: He took off the armour . . .

N2: Collected five smooth stones and off he went.

Scene 4: The fight

N1: Goliath saw him coming and threw back his head and laughed.

Goliath: They've sent out a scrap for the birds!

N2: Goliath lumbered down the hill.

N1: David ran towards Goliath.

David: It is you who'll be food for the birds! My God will deliver you into my hands today.

N2: Goliath came on.

N1: David stopped. He whirled his sling round and round.

N2: The stone flew straight . . .

N1: Straight into Goliath's forehead.

(*Goliath's shadow collapses*)

N2: For a minute there was silence.

N1: Then a cheer went up from the army of Israel.

N2: The Philistine army ran away.

N1: The Israelites chased after them. They had won!

Leader: Goliath was a big problem, but David believed that God was bigger still and could help him. Christians believe that God is bigger than any problem and that he can help in difficult situations.

Follow up

The children could draw or paint themselves when feeling frightened, upset or anxious. These could form the starting point for discussion of what can be done to help.

Ask the children to write down anonymously a fear they have or something that upsets them on a slip of paper. Redistribute them and ask each child to read what is written. Record the kind of fear eg fear of animals, the dark, school tests etc. Talk with the children about what helps when they are afraid etc. Examples might be having someone to talk to, being with friends, sitting quietly on their own etc.

Consider children who show bravery, eg those fighting serious illness or handicap. How do they view the world? How can they be helped to win their battles?

Look at the story of Anne Frank.

Many people have carried out difficult tasks believing that this was what God wanted them to do (eg Dr Barnardo, Brother Andrew). See the *Faith in Action* series, published by RMEP.

Look at well known Bible stories where leading characters took risks eg Joshua (Joshua 5), and Gideon (Judges 6–7). Look at the risks they took and how (if at all) they were minimised.

Rewrite the ending as if the risk had been avoided.

Watch the video 'David the Shepherd King' produced by Scripture Union.

10   Choices

Aim

To look at the decision made by Peter to follow Jesus and to think about the choices we make.

Bible base

Matthew 4:18–22. Jesus calls four fishermen. It would be easy to assume that when Peter met Jesus whilst fishing he made a snap decision to follow him. However John 1:35–42 shows us that the fishermen already knew Jesus and believed him to be the Messiah.

Class Preparation

Talk about choosing. What things are they allowed the choose? Keep a record for a day of all the choices they have to make eg what to have for breakfast, etc.

Conduct a class survey of choice of favourite pets, food, fruit etc. and display the results on a graph. Everyone could give three reasons for their choices.

Talk about choices which are quick and easy and those which affect our lives. What things influence the decisions we make? Look at some common situations that require decisions eg a friend wants you to go to the cinema rather than visit your gran, what to wear to a party etc. Ask them to try and identify the steps they go through to make a decision.

Look at the story of Peter choosing to follow Jesus – what would we have had to consider in making that decision? Role-play situations where they have to make decisions.

Presentation

Leader: Every day we make all sorts of choices – listen to some of these . . .

(Children relate some of their choices or they act out some of their role-playing situations eg. deciding whether to hand in a £5 note they find on the ground, whether to go to the cinema or to see their gran)

Leader: The following is a story about a girl who made a choice . . .

Narrator: Elizabeth lived in a large house and had lots of toys. She had a special coat which she prized above everything else – it was beautifully made and had six different coloured buttons. It was nearing her tenth birthday when her father sent for her.

Father: Tomorrow it is your birthday – you will be ten years old.

Narrator: As if she needed reminding!

Father: When you were a baby we held a huge party for you and people brought you many presents. However there was one old lady who didn't bring anything – she said she would return in ten years when you could choose your own present.

Elizabeth: How exciting! I wonder what I should choose – a new bike, a TV set, a computer . . .

Narrator: The next day when she was playing in the garden an old lady was standing before her holding her coat.

Old Lady: Each of these buttons represents a gift – you can choose just one of them. The green button means you will be very wealthy, the red one means you can have all the latest games and toys, the blue button will give you brains. The yellow one will provide all the friends you could ever want. The orange button will give you long and healthy life while this purple one will give you a kind heart.

Elizabeth: Do I have to choose right away?

Old Lady: No, I will return at sunset and you can tell me then.

Narrator: The old lady disappeared and Elizabeth was left

46

thinking about her decision.

Elizabeth: It would be excellent to have a room full of toys, but then again it would be good to be so clever I didn't need to go to school. If I had lots of money I could buy my own toys, but then maybe people would only like me for my money. Perhaps I'll choose the yellow one so that I can have loads of friends.

Narrator: The day wore on and Elizabeth was still thinking . . .

Elizabeth: It would be good never to be ill, but would that make me really happy? I can't remember what the purple button stood for. It can't have been very important.

Old Lady: Elizabeth!

Elizabeth: You look worn out, do sit down. I'll go and make you a cup of tea.

Old Lady: (*When Elizabeth returns*): You have chosen well!

Elizabeth: But I haven't chosen yet!

Old Lady: Toys, wealth, health, friends, brains are not the most important and they won't make you happy. A kind heart will bring you great happiness and it will also make others happy.

Narrator: Elizabeth suddenly remembered the purple button was the gift of a kind heart. It was the best present she could have and it had already started to work.

Leader: Elizabeth made a good choice in that story. The Bible tells us that Simon Peter also had to make a choice. He had to decide whether to follow Jesus. It can't have been easy for him to decide – he had a lot to lose – his job and his home. However even though Jesus didn't offer him wealth or a home Peter decided that Jesus was worth following. So did the other disciples. This is what happened. (*Children act out the following . . .*)

Narrator: As Jesus walked along the shore on Lake Galilee, he saw two fishermen. They were brothers and their names were Simon Peter and Andrew. Jesus called out . . .

Jesus: Come with me and I will teach you to catch men.

Narrator: At once they left their nets and went with him. He went on and saw two other brothers James and John. They were in their boat with their father Zebedee, getting their nets ready. Jesus called them and at once they left the

47

boat and their father and went with him.

Leader: Some choices we make, like what to have for breakfast, are quick and easy. Others, like the one Simon Peter made, can affect our whole lives.

Follow up

Make some board games, mazes or puzzles about making choices.

Write or read stories which involve choosing your own adventure, eg the Make Your Own Adventure series by Karen King, published by Scripture Union.

Think about choices which can be risky and plan responses.

Make a list of personal choices which the children can add to when they wish eg Today I decided to tidy my desk.

(Other ideas on decision-making can be found in the second outline for Lent.)

11 'I' Disease

Aim

To show that God is a loving father, ready to forgive people.

Bible base

Luke 15:11–32. The lost son. Jesus told this parable to tax collectors and other outcasts (along with those of the lost sheep and the lost coin, also found in Luke 15) to show God's attitude to these people. This was in sharp contrast to the Pharisees who despised them.

Pigs were considered unclean animals by the Jews and this was why the idea of tending the pigs was so abhorrent to the son. The parallel of the loving father may need to be treated sensitively.

Preparation

Ask the children if they have ever run away from home, (or at least wanted to).

Read or tell the story of the boy who left home from Luke 15:11–24 and explain that God is like the father in the story.

The children could rewrite the story as a modern version eg the father owns a toy factory, the son leaves and spends all his money on 'friends' and discos etc.

Find out which animals are regarded as unclean or sacred in different countries and why.

Make puppets ready for the assembly ie the father, the two sons, pigs, servants. Alternatively, use circular cards painted with different faces.

Presentation

Leader: How many of you have visited the optician? When you go you are asked to read a chart of letters. (*Have a chart prepared and ask children in various parts of the hall to read a line.*) People sometimes need glasses to help them see better. Sometimes it is because they have an eye disease.

Child 1: But everyone here has 'I' disease, not something wrong with their eyes but this . . .

Child 2: 'I' don't want to make my bed.

Child 3: 'I' don't want to wash up.

Child 4: 'I'm not going to do that!

Leader: We all have times when we think only about ourselves and how we feel. Our story today is about someone just like that.

(*Use the puppets to tell the story. Set up some sort of box behind which the children can hide, eg a table on its side.*)

Narrator: Jesus told this story about a man who had two sons. One worked hard but the younger brother was fed up with working on the farm. He went to his father and said . . .

Younger son: When you die I will get some of your money. Why not give it to me now, so that I can travel a bit and enjoy myself?

Father: Do you really want to leave all the family and your home?

Younger son: Yes. All we do here is work. I want to go and meet different people and have fun.

Father(*sadly*): Well, if that's what you want, I won't stand in your way.

Narrator: The father got the money together and gave it to his younger son.

Father: Here you are. Don't waste it, remember this is your share. I have nothing more to give you.

Narrator: The young man packed his things and set off. He went to live in a country far away and spent his money on new clothes, parties and everything he wanted. He soon made lots of friends, people who were ready to help him spend his money. Everything seemed to be going his way. Then one day, his money ran out.

Younger son: I'll ask my friends to lend me some money.

50

They're bound to help me, I've done so much for them.

1st friend: Oh, I'm sorry. You've caught me at a bad time, I don't get paid until the end of the month.

2nd friend: Oh no, you've run out of money! That's bad luck, I don't suppose you'll be throwing any more parties. See you around!

Narrator: Not one of his friends would help him. He was left very much alone.

Younger son: I must find a job so that I can at least eat. Excuse me, sir, do you have any work for me?

Farmer: As it happens, my herdsman has just left. You can look after my pigs.

Younger son: What? Me look after pigs? You can't be serious!

Farmer: Suit yourself. That's all I have to offer.

Younger son: (*hesitates*): Well . . . I suppose I don't have much choice.

Narrator: So the son went to look after the pigs. But that year the country was very short of food and the young man was so hungry he wanted to eat the pigs' food. Then he began to think.

Younger son: I'm stupid. Here I am with nothing to eat while in my father's house everyone has plenty. I must have been mad to leave home . . . I know what I'll do! I'll go home and tell my father that I was wrong. I'll tell him how sorry I am, and ask him to let me work as a servant. I certainly don't deserve to be treated as a son any more.

Narrator: So the son began the long walk home, ragged and dirty and weak with hunger. He dreaded meeting his father. But his father spotted him coming and ran to meet him.

Father: I've missed you so much. I've been worrying about you. I've been looking out for you every day.

Younger son: I'm sorry, I've done wrong.

Narrator: His father threw his arms around his son.

Father: Come quickly, everyone. My son has returned! Bring him some new clothes and prepare a huge party. We're going to celebrate. I thought I had lost my son but now I've found him.

Narrator: Jesus said God is like that father. When those who have done wrong come back to him and say they are sorry, God is glad and forgives them. Another way of telling the story is by giving a number of children in the class different types of sweet wrappers which can be used in the narrative. For example:

Reader 1: A man had two sons. One was fed up with working on the farm and wanted his share of the *'bounty'*.

Reader 2: He set off on a long journey. He walked, for there were no *'double deckers'* in those days.

Reader 3: He was rich and so he joined the *'smartie'*, set.

Reader 4: However he soon ran out of money which put an end to his *'revels'*.

Reader 5: His so-called friends deserted him and he became a *'drifter'*.

Reader 6: Whilst looking after pigs he was so hungry he was just about to *'chomp'* into their food.

Reader 7: As he looked up at the *'galaxy'*

Reader 8: Where he saw *'Mars'* and the *'Milky Way'*

Reader 9: He said, 'I've been a complete and *'whole nut''* and he decided to go home.

Reader 10: When he arrived back his father was delighted to see him and called for new clothes, the best food and the *'golden cup'*.

Reader 11: 'My son has come back and today we are going to have a *'feast'*, he said.

As the children say their line they produce the appropriate wrapper. Further details can be added depending on what sweets you can find!

Follow up

Discuss the effects of the son's selfishness on his father, his brother and the rest of the household.

Discuss with the children any ways they are selfish as well as any occasions when they have offered to help in some way.

Look at the story *The Lion, the Witch and the Wardrobe* by C S Lewis. Draw up a list of the ways Edmund was selfish and the consequences that his selfishness had.

Look at the other two parables in Luke 15, the lost sheep and the lost coin, and compare the three. How are they alike and how different?

Discuss the various ways of using money. How do the children use their money now?

Section 2   Our Friends and Others

12   So who is my friend?

Aim

To introduce the theme of friendship.

Bible base

Luke 10:25–37. The parable of the Good Samaritan. This story shows that helping each other is important and that it is not who you are, or what you say that matters but what you do. The priest and the Levite were important respected people, and they thought they were doing right, but it was the Samaritan who proved himself to be the true neighbour, or friend.

Class preparation

This group of assemblies is on the theme of friendship and so the class activity can be used in several outlines.

Brainstorm on the word friend.

Discuss with the children why they have friends and what they do with them.

Ask the children to list all the friends they have including imaginary friends and grown-ups.

Make a 'friend' wordbox.

How could you be a friend to someone you don't like? Jesus told a story showing how we should behave to others. (Explain that Jews and Samaritans were enemies.) Read and discuss the Good Samaritan story. Look particularly at the responses of the outsiders and passers-by.

Collect or write poems about friends and friendship.

Presentation

Leader: Our class have been looking at friends. Here are some poems we've written (or found) about friends.
(*Children read poems.*)
Jesus told a story about someone who needed a friend. We are going to act it for you.
(*One group mimes while the other group reads the various parts.*)

Friends:
'Don't do it John, don't go it alone,
You know what they say of that track.
You've heard on the news, take heed of our views,
Or you may not be coming back.'

John:
'I must get to Jericho pronto, at once,
I can't hang around any longer.
I've got to be quick, my brother is sick,
And he isn't getting much stronger.'

Friends:
'Take care as you go, whatever you do,
There are muggers behind every rock.'

John:
'I hear what you say, but I'll be OK,
Those thieves could be in for a shock.'

Narrator:
He hadn't gone far from the lights of the town,
In fact they were just out of sight,
When with barely a sound, he was knocked to the ground,
And given no chance of a fight.

He lay there and wished he had heeded the word,
Of his friends he had left in the town.
He knew he would die, unless someone passed by,
And the blood from his wounds trickled down.

At last he heard footsteps, help was at hand.
A priest on his way to the city.
But he had one glance, didn't take any chance,
And rushed off, without showing pity.

John just lay there, and groaned in his pain,
There seemed no end to his misery.
A Levite passed by, and avoided his eye,
And John thought about his obituary!

It was hot in the sun, the end was not far,
When Sam came along on his donkey.

Good Samaritan:
'What's up old chap, have you had a mishap?
That leg of yours looks kind of wonkey!'

Narrator:
He lifted John up on his two litre mule,
And patched up his wounds with a hanky.

Good Samaritan:
'We'll soon have you right, you can stop overnight,
At a motel I know, rather swanky.'

Narrator:
As morning arrived so Sam packed up his bags,
And said to the man at reception,

Good Samaritan:
'To aid his progress, charge American Express,
I'll settle it all, no exception.'

Jesus:
'Who was the neighbour to John?' Jesus asked,

56

'Who acted just like a brother?'

Friends:
'Why Sam was the one, who aided poor John'

Jesus:
'Now you act the same with each other!'

Leader: Think for a moment of someone you could show friendship to today.

Follow up

Look at other stories of friendship in the Bible eg David and Jonathan (1 Samuel 17:55–18:16, 19:1–20:42), David and Mephibosheth (2 Samuel 9:1–13).
   Write an advert for yourself as a friend.
   Write a story about a lonely child who finds a new friend.

13   Neighbours

Aim

This is a second assembly based on the story of the Good Samaritan. It could be used as a follow up to the previous outline.

Presentation

Introduction: Play a recording of the theme song from the TV programme *'Neighbours'*.
The following is performed as a mimed drama to narrative.

Narrator:
David and his parents had only arrived in the town the week before term started. There had been no time to get to know any other children at his new school and David was worried about his first morning. He didn't know where to go, who anyone was and most of all he had no friends. He really missed Kevin and James from his old school.

There seemed to be so many children in the playground, and, as a first year, he felt so much smaller than most of them. He slowly crept his way round the edge, keeping close to the school building, trying very hard not to be noticed. He was carrying his new school bag which had his pencil case and dinner money in it.

Passing a doorway, he saw a small group of much older children. They were talking about a film they had seen on the telly the night before. Just as David thought he had gone past without being noticed, he heard one of the group say, 'Here's a new kid. Let's see what he's got in his bag.'

'Here, new kid, empty out your bag!'

David was terrified and turned to run. Before he had gone far two of the bigger boys had grabbed him. 'Don't you like being with us?' asked one of them as they dragged him back to the gang. One of the girls tore the bag from David and unzipped the opening.

'Here, look what I've found,' she said, holding up David's PE shorts. 'You'll look real new in them – I think we'd better make them look a bit older.' She dropped them in a muddy puddle and jumped on them, splashing the others in the group.

'Here, watch what you're doing, kid,' shouted one of the boys. 'You've just soaked me.'

The gang tipped all David's things out onto the playground. They opened his pencil case and took his pen. They found his dinner money and shared that out between them. When David tried to grab it back he was pushed over.

'Just take a little rest while we sort this out,' said another of the boys.

After a bit they all lost interest and drifted away, leaving David sitting on the ground desperately collecting what was left of the contents of his bag. He started to cry as he realised that with no dinner money he would go hungry for the day.

As he was picking up the empty pencil case a group of girls walked by, chatting about Jason Donovan. One of them looked down at David and said, 'You can't sit around here all day you know. You have to work at this school. You new kids – you're so lazy.' All the others thought this was really funny and they all went off laughing.

David lifted his PE shorts out of the puddle and was squeezing them to get the water out. From behind him he heard a voice.

'Don't you know that your bag should be left in school before you come out to play? You really must learn the school rules. Anyway, I'm late for the Staff Meeting – for goodness sake get your things together before the whistle blows.' And off went one of the teachers.

David was wishing that the family had never moved here that he had never come to this horrible school, and most of all that someone would help him. He had collected all his things – well, all those that were left, and was trying to brush the dust from his trousers.

'Hi,' said a girl's voice. 'Haven't you just moved into number 62?'

'Er, yes,' said David.

'Well, I live at 58 and I thought I saw you when you arrived.' Suddenly all went quiet in the playground as the whistle was blown. 'Come on then,' said the girl. 'I'll show you where to go – Mrs. Johnson said there was a new boy in our class.'

Bible reading: Luke 10:29–37

'Neighbours' theme music.

14   A true friend is . . .

Aim

To show how, even though Peter let Jesus down, Jesus showed he was a true friend by forgiving him.

Bible base

Luke 22:54–62. Peter denies knowing Jesus.

Preparation

Discuss the qualities of a good friend. Do they choose their friends? Do they ever break friends? Why? Have they ever let a friend down?

Finish the sentence 'A true friend is . . .'

Tell the children the Aesop's fable which is dramatised below and discuss what it shows.

Presentation

Leader: One day two friends, Mike and Sarah, went out for a stroll in the countryside. Mike had a sore leg and so he limped a bit, but they took it slowly and it didn't stop them enjoying themselves.

(*The two friends comment to each other on the beautiful scenery, stop to have a picnic etc.*)

Leader: All was going well until suddenly from behind the bushes (*children can be used as bushes and trees*) a large bear appeared, growling fiercely, intent upon finding some lunch.

(*Bear sniffs around*)

On seeing the bear, Sarah decided she didn't want to hang around and make polite conversation, so she found the nearest tree and scrambled up. (*Sarah climbs on a chair behind a group of 'trees'*.) Mike, however, couldn't run because of his bad leg. He had to think of something fairly quickly as the bear was getting closer. He'd heard somewhere that if you lay down and pretended you were dead, bears lost interest. It was worth a try . . .

(*Mike lies down and bear comes and sniffs all around his 'dead' body, particularly the ears, loses interest and wanders off.*) When Sarah realised the bear had gone, she came down from the tree.

Sarah: Phew! I'm glad that bear's gone. It got close to you, I thought you'd had it for sure. It was so close it looked as if it was whispering in your ear.

Mike: It did actually! It said that you shouldn't rely on someone who is likely to desert you at the first sign of trouble . . .

(*They go off, Sarah looking perplexed.*)

Leader: Sarah wasn't a very good friend, because she let Mike down. Unfortunately we all let our friends down at some time or other. One of Jesus' friends let him down. Listen to what happened when Jesus was on trial and Peter went to find out what was going on.

Reading: Luke 22: 54–62 (*this could be dramatised*)

Leader: Peter let Jesus down by pretending he didn't know him. That wasn't the end of the story though, as Jesus showed what a good friend he was by forgiving Peter and giving him a second chance.

Follow up

Read to the class *Miles and the Computer* by Taffy Davies, published by Scripture Union, based on the parable of the unforgiving servant (Matthew 18:21–35).

Look at other Aesop fables.

Read the story of the 'Empty Box' about a lady who discovers what true friendship is, found in *'Plays for Assembly'* by Peter M. Allen, published by Schofield and Sims Ltd. This could be dramatised and made into another assembly.

Write a job description for a friend.

Choose a friend. Write down ten things which are the same or very similar for the two of you. Then write down ten things which are different. Discuss these similarities and differences and think about which ones are important to you and why.

Distribute slips of paper. Each child writes (anonymously) one thing that might cause a problem with a friendship. Collect the strips and redistribute them. A child reads out a problem and the others suggest a response.

Make a code of friendship to display in the classroom.

Draw cartoon strips of friends breaking up and how they make up.

Brainstorm 'feeling' words for when a friendship is going well, or deteriorating.

15   Friends in a fiery furnace

Aim

To explore the idea of standing up for what you believe in.

Bible base

Daniel 3. Nebuchadnezzar and his golden statue. This story is set in Babylon during the Exile of the Jews. Shadrach, Meshach and Abednego had become important men in the kingdom and the native officials were jealous. They stood up for their beliefs and got into trouble, but God was able to rescue them.

Preparation

Ask the children about situations when they or their friends are in difficulty or under pressure and need support. Ask them if they have ever had to stand up for what they believe is right. When is this easy (when others agree), when is it hard?
Read the story of Shadrach, Meshach and Abednego in Daniel chapter 3. Why did they make a stand? Talk about the pressure they would have been under to conform. Would it have made any difference that there were three of them?
The children could make their own instruments to represent those mentioned in the story.
A gold statue could also be made out of boxes or collage etc.

Presentation

Participants: Leader, narrator, Nebuchadnezzar, musicians, officials, people of Babylon, guards, angel, herald.

Leader: Have you ever heard someone say, 'Don't be afraid to stand up for what you believe is right?' This means you ought to be brave enough to say and do what you believe in, even if other people don't agree with you. Watch what happens to these three men who stood up for what they knew was right, even though it would get them into trouble.

Their names were Shadrach, Meshach and Abednego, and they lived in a city called Babylon. They weren't born there; they came from Israel, but the king of Babylon had captured Israel and taken many of the people who lived there back to his city. Shadrach, Meshach and Abednego were given the important job of helping rule the city, but some of the Babylonian officials were jealous.

Narrator: King Nebuchadnezzar made a great big golden statue which was thirty metres high and three metres wide. He called together all his governors, mayors, magistrates and officials. The Royal herald made a speech:

Herald: People of all Nations! When you hear the trumpet (*pause after each instrument mentioned so that the musicians can play on cue*), the oboe, the lyre, the zither, the harp, followed by all the other instruments, you must fall down and worship the statue made by King Nebuchadnezzar. If anyone refuses, he will be thrown into the fiery furnace.

Narrator: And so when the trumpet, oboe, lyre, zither, harp and all the other instruments (*they play on cue*) sounded, everyone fell flat on their faces before the gold statue. Everyone, that is, except Shadrach, Meshach and Abednego. The officials saw their chance to get Shadrach, Meshach, and Abednego into trouble. They went to the king.

Officials: May your Majesty live for ever! You have issued an order that as soon as the trumpet, oboe, lyre, zither, harp and all the other instruments play (*they play on cue*) everyone must worship your statue. Well, three man are not!

Narrator: The king was furious and sent for them immediately.

King: Shadrach, Meshach and Abendigo, is it true that you refuse to bow down to my gold statue when you hear the trumpet, oboe, lyre, zither, harp and all the other instruments? (*they play on cue again*) You realise that if you do not obey my commands I have no option but to throw you into the fiery furnace. Do you think your God will save you?

S, M, A: We will obey you in many things, but not this. Our God is greater than any king, even you. If he wants to, he can rescue us from the fire. But even if he doesn't, we still won't worship an idol.

Narrator: Nebuchadnezzar was furious. No-one had ever spoken to him like that before. He shouted to his men . . .

King: Heat the furnace seven times hotter than usual! Then throw these three into it!

Narrator: The king went to watch from a safe distance. More and more wood was thrown on. The flames leapt higher and higher.

(*Children dressed in red and orange or carrying flames could leap around to represent the fire*)

The soldiers tied the hands of Shadrach, Meshach and Abednego and pushed them in. Nebuchadnezzar watched with interest. Suddenly he jumped up.

King: How many men did you throw in?

Guards: Three, your Majesty.

King: But there are four men in there and they are walking around! That fourth one doesn't look very human, he looks like an angel. Come out Shadrach, Meshach and Abednego!

Narrator: They came out. The fire had not touched them! Even their clothes and hair weren't burnt.

King: Praise the God of Shadrach, Meshach and Abednego! He sent his angel to rescue them. They disobeyed my orders and risked their lives rather than bow down to any god but their own. Anyone who says anything against their God shall be torn limb from limb!

Narrator: The Babylonians who had reported the three Jews were afraid and sneaked off. They could not fight against the God of the Jews.

Leader: Everyone thought Shadrach, Meshach and Abednego would die but God looked after them.

(*Children could then say prayers for people who are in prison because of what they believe, and for courage to be true to what you believe*)

Follow up

Read another story from the book of Daniel about Daniel in the lions' pit. (Daniel 3)

Find out about dissidents and political prisoners in various parts of the world. Have a debate about whether people should be put in prison for what they think. Include an example where they should.

Look up some of the people in the New Testament who suffered because of their faith in Jesus. Acts 7 – Stephen, Acts 12 – Peter, Acts 16:16–40 – Paul.

Discuss when people need to have faith in God and/or themselves.

Discuss how it feels when other people turn their back on you because of what you believe, think or say.

Draw two webs, one of feelings and the other of what helps eg Sticking by what is right, knowing God still cares, your family helps etc.

16 Abraham sets off into the unknown

Aim

To explore the theme of trust and to show that Abraham trusted God enough to follow him into the unknown.

Bible base

Genesis 12:1–9. God calls Abraham

Preparation

Tell the children that they are going on a long journey. They should imagine they have a suitcase in front of them and act out packing the case with things that they will need for the journey. Set off together asking if any of them know where they are going, if they have got a map etc. Talk about what they might be seeing on the way, who they have left behind, how they are feeling. After a few minutes explain that you have arrived and pretend to set up camp. Ask how they feel now that they have arrived.

Draw a parallel with the above activity and the story of Abraham's journey (Genesis 12:1–9). Show on a map where this happened.

Explore the theme of trust. Play some trust games under careful supervision! Eg 1. In pairs one is blindfolded and the other leads his/her partner around obstacles. 2. Put three chairs out in a row. Blindfold a volunteer and stand them on the first chair. Get them to walk on to the second and third chairs. Then ask them to step onto a fourth chair which has been placed there without them knowing. Make the point that sometimes we have to put our trust in something we cannot see.

Talk about things that they put their trust in and people in whom they trust.

Presentation

Leader: Today we are thinking about trust. I'd like a volunteer who trusts me.

At this point use one of the trust exercises from above. If the first one is used, children from the class could position themselves to form an obstacle course. Ask the volunteer how easy they found it to trust.

Leader: Sometimes it is easier to trust than other times. The following is a story about a man called Blondin. He asked someone to trust him.

Narrator: Blondin was renowned for his amazing and daring feats across a tightrope. One day he was entertaining a crowd as he crossed the Niagara Falls on the tightrope.

(Here one child walks across a rope or upside down form, using a snooker cue as his balance.)

The crowd *(some of the other children)* gasped in wonder as first he walked across with a pole and then he took a wheelbarrow over *(this is acted out)*. But then the crowd was silenced as Blondin said . . .

Blondin: Do I have a volunteer to be carried across in my wheelbarrow?

Narrator: There wasn't a murmur from the crowd until one little girl piped up.

Girl: I'll come!

Narrator: There was a hush as slowly Blondin wheeled the little girl across. Everyone held their breath. Would they make it? Great sighs of relief and cheers echoed around as they reached the other side. One of the crowd asked . . .

Crowd member: Why did you volunteer?

Girl: I always trust my daddy.

Leader: The little girl trusted Blondin because she knew him and knew he wouldn't let her down. In the same way as the girl trusted her father there are a number of stories in the Bible about people who trusted God. Two of these are

Abraham and Sarah.

If you have a free standing tent, have it set up to one side, with a couple of children who are Abraham and Sarah sitting inside. They come out.

Abraham: Hello, I'm Abraham and this is my wife, Sarah.

Sarah. God told us to pack up all our belongings and leave our city.

Abraham: We didn't know where we were going, but God said he would lead us to a better land, that he would make my name famous and that we would have lots of children.

Sarah: Our family and friends thought we were mad, although our nephew Lot came with us.

Abraham: We had some adventures along the way, I can tell you. God kept his word though. He showed us the way until we reached Canaan, the promised land. I'm also glad to say that I had many descendants!

Leader: Abraham and Sarah discovered that God was trustworthy. Think about those people whom you can trust and be thankful for them.

Follow up

Look at maps and plot the places where the children have lived. Discuss reasons why people move. How would they feel if they had to move next week? Talk about reasons for and against moving. Compare them with any Abraham may have had.

Think about people who may be in the news who are moving and look at the reasons. Collect newspaper pictures and try to imagine how the people might be feeling.

17   Joseph and his brothers

Aim

To introduce the theme of bullying by looking at the story of Joseph and his brothers.

Bible base

Genesis 37 and 42–46. Joseph and his brothers.

Preparation

In pairs get the children to talk about three differences between them eg hair colour, height, family, and three things that they have in common.

Talk about boasting and how people react to it.

Discuss jealousy. What makes them jealous? How do they show it?

Work in pairs. Write to an imaginary problem page in a magazine about a bullying problem that might happen in school. Give the problem to another pair of children and let them write a reply underneath.

Have a general discussion on 'bullying' (in its broadest sense). Have they seen anyone bullied at school? If you were being bullied, would you tell someone? Why do you think children call each other names?

Read and discuss parts of *Terry on the fence* by Bernard Ashley, published by Puffin eg Terry on the bandstand in the park and his eventual work for the gang. Also *The Eighteenth Emergency* by Betsy Byars, Bodley Head eg Hammerman as a caveman and the fight at the end.

Do some role-play where people are ganging up on someone in an everyday situation and how the victim handles it. It could be done several times with the same gang and same character showing different ways of handling it. eg where he hits out and gets beaten up, where he firmly decides not to give in, where he gives in.

Look at the story of Joseph – how he treated his brothers and vice versa. Look at how their relationship changed.

Presentation

Time traveller: Today we are going to transport you back in time to watch an incident that happened a long time ago. (*More of an introduction could be added here with the time travellers explaining who they are etc.*)

(*Play some 'space' music*)

(*A boy is crouching in a 'pit' whimpering. In come ten others talking and arguing with each other.*)

Time traveller 2: I wonder what's going on here? Perhaps these men will rescue him from the pit.

TT 1: They might, let's watch and see.

Brother 1: He's had enough now – you don't really want to kill him . . .

Brother 2: We certainly do!

Brother 3: Let's be done with the dreamer.

Brother 4: No-one will ever know what's happened to him.

Brother 5: We can say we never saw him.

(*They start muttering about a very colourful garment*)

Brother 1: Let's leave it for the moment and get something to eat. (*They go off*)

TT 1: Oh, I think I understand what is happening now. That boy in the pit is a rich man's son and these men are robbers who've waylaid him and taken his belongings and they're talking about murdering him!

(*The brothers return except Brother 1*)

Brother 2: I still say we should kill him. I'm fed up with the way he is always boasting.

Brother 6: Yes, it's not fair. He's always been father's favourite.

Brother 7: That's why he got this fancy coat.

Brother 8: What about those dreams he has of him lording it over us? That'll be the day!

TT2: I don't believe it! They're not bandits, they're his brothers!

TT1: They must be very jealous and fed up with him if they want to kill him.

Brother 9: I've got an idea! Here come some merchants on their way to Egypt. Why don't we sell him as a slave, then we can make some money as well as getting rid of him.

(Brothers agree, traders come on and the deal is struck)

TT 1: Poor thing, I wonder what will happen to him now.

TT 2: I guess we'll have to wait until another day to find out!

Narrator: You can find out what happened to Joseph and his brothers by reading the rest of this story in the Bible. There was wrong on both sides of this story – Joseph in the pit was a nuisance at home and very spoilt, but his brothers went too far in trying to get rid of him. As Joseph grew up he was able to forgive his brothers. Even though this is an old story it could have happened today . . .

(Tape of Newsround theme music)

Interviewer *(with microphone)*: Welcome to another edition of *Newsround*. A survey has revealed that one out of five children has been bullied. Let's hand over to our reporter at the local school.

Reporter: Wouldn't the world be a boring place if everyone was the same! One of the problems is that some people won't accept that others are different, so they pick on these differences. In class we have looked at our similarities and differences. This is what we discovered.

(A few children read out some that they found, based on the class work).

Reporter: Here are some modern day examples of situations where someone is being picked on.

(Here some of the role plays could be acted out by groups of children.)

Comment *(by teacher possibly)*: Joseph chose to forgive his brothers for picking on him. Sometimes, even though it is hard, we need to forgive people for being nasty to us.

Follow up

Pretend to be one of Joseph's brothers and write to a problem page.

Rewrite the ending of the story of Joseph and his brothers imagining what might have happened if Joseph had not forgiven his brothers.

Draw a cartoon strip where someone is being annoyed and show how they handle it well or badly.

Read *Tusk, Tusk* by David McKee, published by Andersen Press.

Watch the video *Joseph* produced by Scripture Union, for the whole story about Joseph and his brothers.

18 The rescue of Moses

Aim

To look at the rescue of Moses as a baby and to highlight the issue of discrimination.

Bible base

Exodus 1:8 – 2:10 Moses in the bulrushes. The Pharaoh was feeling threatened by the growing number of Israelites. By killing all their baby boys he hoped to reduce the Israelites' potential power. Moses, however, was protected in a special way; he was saved for a purpose.

Preparation

Play a game which involves discrimination against people wearing certain colours. Have enough cards for everyone, with instructions which say things like, 'ignore anyone wearing red,' 'make a face at anyone in blue'. They can be repeated if necessary. Give them five minutes to discover as many of the other rules of discrimination as they can, whilst still following the rule on their card.

Alternatively divide the class into two groups for any arbitrary reason eg those who have brown hair and those who don't. Make those with brown hair work longer. Reverse the roles. Explain what you have been doing.

For both situations it is very important to discuss how the children felt and give them a chance to release their feelings.

Explain that we don't normally react in such an irrational way towards colour. So why do we react negatively towards people who are different? Brainstorm for barriers such as race, language, age, handicap. Who is it most difficult to make friends with? Why? How could such barriers be overcome?

Ask the children to cut out magazine pictures of as many different people as possible. Discuss why they are different.

Look to see how differences are represented in the media. Look for any stories currently in the news where people are being discriminated against.

Look at the story of Moses' escape from death. Talk about why the Pharaoh acted as he did. How else could he have reacted? Practise the story as a play.

Presentation

Leader: We have been looking at various ways people are discriminated against. These are some of the stories currently in the news where people are being maltreated because they are different.

(*Here some examples can be read out*)

But the problem is not a new one. People have been discriminated against for thousands of years. Here is one such story from the Bible.

Narrator: Long ago, when Egypt was a great and powerful nation, the Pharaoh of the land became worried. The Israelites were living in Egypt and they seemed to be growing in number.

Pharaoh: Look at all these Israelites. There are hundreds of them. One day they may rise up against us and fight us. They may even drive us out of the land. We must do something about them. Set them to work! Make them slaves! They can build my new cities and work on the pyramids.

Narrator: So it happened that the Israelites worked from dawn until dusk. If they did not work hard, they were whipped. But still the numbers of the Israelites continued to grow until one day Pharaoh could stand it no longer.

Pharaoh: Every baby boy that is born to the Israelites must be killed. Throw them into the River Nile! Only the girls may live.

Narrator: The Israelites were shocked and terrified. What could they do? Among the Israelites was a couple who loved and worshipped God, Jochabed and Amram. They already had two children, Miriam and Aaron. Just after the Pharaoh had made his law they had another baby. It was a boy!

Jochabed: My poor baby. What shall we do, Amram? We must protect him.

Amram: We will hide him from the soldiers.

Narrator: For three months they kept the baby hidden. But after this time, he could be hidden no longer.

Jochabed: We must find somewhere else to hide our baby. The soldiers will come soon and find him. What shall we do?

Miriam: I know, we could hide him among the bulrushes by the river. I will watch him so that no harm comes to him.

Aaron: That's a good idea.

Amram: Let's make a basket out of reeds. We must cover it with tar to make sure it is waterproof.

Miriam: Put a soft cushion in, so that the baby is comfortable.

Narrator: So they worked hard to make a basket. The next time the soldiers came near, Jochabed took the special basket to the water's edge and put it among the bulrushes. The cradle floated but it did not move. Miriam stayed close by to watch. After a while Pharaoh's daughter came down to the river to bathe. Miriam held her breath as the baby started to cry.

Princess: What's that noise? It sounds like a baby crying. Go and take a look.

Maid (*returning with basket*): It is a baby, your Highness. I think he must be hungry.

Princess: I think he is an Israelite baby. My father is too cruel sometimes. I'd like to look after it.

Narrator: Miriam saw her opportunity and rushed up.

Miriam: Would you like me to get a nurse for you? I know someone who would look after him.

Princess: Yes, please. Can you do it straight away?

Miriam: Mother, mother! The princess has found our baby. Come quickly!

Princess: Would you take care of this baby for me please? When he is old enough, you may bring him to the palace and I will adopt him as my son.

Jochabed: Of course I will, thank you very much. Do you have a name for him?

Princess: I will name him Moses because I lifted him out of the water. That is what Moses means.

Narrator: So Moses was looked after by his parents until he was old enough to go to the palace. All that time God took care of him because in the future he had a great work for Moses to do.

Follow up

Other assemblies on a similar theme are Fruit Parade, So who is my friend? Joseph and his brothers.

Discuss why people find it difficult to accept others from other areas of the country or world.

Look at Jesus' reaction to people who were normally victims of prejudice eg Matthew 12:9–14 and 15:21–28, Mark 10:13–16 and Luke 18:35–43 and 19:1–10. Discuss who was prejudiced against and why.

Look also at assembly on hands where Jesus heals the leper.

Watch 'Exodus', a video produced by Scripture Union, for this and the next part of the story.

This is a complex issue and obviously not something that can be covered in just one assembly and the follow-up. However, it is important to think about discrimination and its effects and to come up with ways that would tackle the topic in all aspects of the curriculum.

19   Joshua and the battle of Jericho

Aim

To use the story of Joshua's victory to think about the importance of working together as a team.

Bible Base

Joshua 6:1–23. The fall of Jericho.

Preparation

Play a team game such as football, netball or volleyball. Afterwards talk about tactics and the need for team-work. There may have been times when they did not work together and the other team scored, or they may need to be congratulated on the way they worked together.
Think of situations where it is important to work together eg orchestra, army.
Ask them to imagine in each case what would happen if they did not work together. Write stories about the disorganised army, the out-of-tune orchestra, the worst football team in the world.
Look at the story of the fall of Jericho. Would Joshua have had the same effect on the people of Jericho if he had walked around the walls alone? Was it important that everyone went?

Presentation

Some of the class act out the part of the people of Jericho. The others are the Israelites.

Leader: Today we're looking at a story from the Bible where team-work was vital.

Narrator 1: A long, long time ago,

Narrator 2: So long that even your parents and teachers weren't born.

(*Rest of class say 'Phew!'*)

1: Yes, a *long* time ago!

2: Hundreds of years ago in the land we now know as Palestine there was a great walled city called Jericho.

(*A number of children holding walls made of card group together.*)

Narrator 3: It was one of the strongest cities in the land and its people knew that they were safe inside, because the great walls were strong, hard and very thick.

1: Not many miles from the city of Jericho ran the river Jordan.

2: And just over on the other side of the Jordan was camped a huge group of people – a bigger crowd than you'd find at Old Trafford, supporting Manchester United,

3: A crowd so big that it even out-numbered the supporters of Liverpool.

1: This crowd were known as the people of Israel. They had been led out of slavery in Egypt by Moses, their leader.

(*Class as crowd chant 'Moses!'*) Mos_{~} Clap Clap clap ...

2: But sadly Moses had died and now Joshua was their leader.

(*Class chant 'Joshua!'*) Joshua clap clap clap.

3: Joshua was now ready to lead the people into the promised land.

(*Crowd: 'Our promised Land. . . . Our promised what?'*)

1: Your promised land. In the desert, as they wandered around for 40 years (*Crowd – 'wander . . . wander . . . wander'*) God promised them that they could have the land of Canaan for their very own.

2: As long as they lived his ways . . . and obeyed his laws.

(*Crowd 'we promise'*)

3: And now they were preparing to cross the River Jordan,

step into Canaan, and fight to take cities. They were a fear-some army,
(*Crowd – 'After you, no, after you old chap!*)
1: And the people of Jericho were scared stiff
(*The people of Jericho stand with knees knocking*)
2: Because they had heard that God was on the people of Israel's side, and that made a big difference.
3: One morning Joshua stood up and told the people the fight plan.
(*Joshua stands up, crowd sits down*)
1: (*As Joshua's voice*) Now listen chaps and chapesses. We've been walking round the desert a long time, haven't we?
And we've got really fit, haven't we?
And we're ready to fight, aren't we?
Well the good news is . . . (*crowd 'yes?'*)
We don't have to . . . (*crowd 'we don't?'*)
1: No, God's told us that he's going to fight *for* us. All we have to do is walk – and we know how to do that, don't we?
(*Crowd 'yes'*) because we've been doing it for 40 years!
(*Crowd gets up and starts walking on the spot*)
2: And so over the Jordan they went and set foot on their promised land.
3: They stopped for a prayer . . . (*crowd kneel and pray*)
1: Then went on towards Jericho.
2: The next day they did what Joshua told them to do.
3: They marched round the city once.
1: Back to camp please!
2: The next day they did what Joshua had told them to do.
3: They marched round the city once.
1: Back to camp please!
2: The next day, the next day, the next day, the next day . . .
3: They marched round the city once.
1: Back to camp please!
2: The next day . . .
3: Joshua stood up and said . . .
1: Now listen, chaps and chapesses . . . I know you've done a lot of walking lately but today is different!
(*Crowd 'Hooray!'*)
We're not going to walk round the city once!
(*Crowd – 'Hooray!'*)

No! God's told us to walk round seven times!
(*Crowd – 'Oh no!'*)
Yes, I know you've all got blisters but be brave!
2: So off they went, and marched round Jericho seven times!
3: Meanwhile, in the city, people were puzzled.
1: On the first day, when the Israelites had walked round the city once, the people in Jericho had wondered what was happening.
2: On the second, third, fourth, fifth and sixth day they had been so curious that they had all come onto the walls to have a good look.
3: On the seventh day they were all there, on top of the walls.
1: They couldn't wait to see what happened next. The ice cream sellers were doing a roaring trade!
2: Ice cream sellers?
1: Yes, you know, Walls of Jericho!
3: So the people of Israel were marching round
2: And there were the people of Jericho looking down.
3: Joshua stood up and said . . .
1: You'll be pleased to know that we haven't got to walk round in circles any more! We've done what God wanted and now all we have to do is shout – nice and loud – and God will give us the city. So get ready, I'll count to three – then you shout.
2: Meanwhile, up on the walls everyone was leaning over wondering what was going on. They'd got a bit dizzy following the people of Israel going round in circles.
3: But now Joshua shouted 1..2..3..And the people of Israel shouted – louder than they'd ever shouted before.
1: The walls began to shiver . . .
2: The walls began to shake . . .
3: and so did the people inside Jericho . . .
1: And particularly those on top of the walls . . .
2: For quite simply, sort of basically, what was happening was that . . . well . . . believe it or not . . . I know it's incredible . . .
3: But the walls fell flat!
1: In marched the Israelites; the city was theirs!
(*Crowd – 'We did it!'*)
2: Excuse me . . . *You* did it?

Everyone kneels. Joshua says 1..2..3..'Thanks, God!'
Leader: If the people of Israel had not acted together they would not have been able to take the city of Jericho. They worked together as a team and trusted in God. Perhaps we could take a leaf out of the Israelites' book!

Follow up

Ask the children to think of something they could achieve by working together which they could not manage alone.

Older children could list the emotions which the people of Jericho might have felt (eg. curiosity, anger, fear, uncertainty, concern about food and water supplies).

Read in the next part of Joshua (ch. 7) what happened when the Israelites didn't obey what God had told them to do, and one man started disobeying the rules. You could work out another play for an assembly based on this episode of the story.

20   Special people

Aim

To look at people who are special to the children and show that Jesus is special to Christians.

Bible base

Mark 14:3–9
The woman anointing Jesus in this story is Mary, the sister of Martha and Lazarus. Anointing was a common custom at feasts, but the woman's action expressed her deep devotion to Jesus.
Mark 4:35–41
The calming of the storm demonstrates the power of Jesus over creation. By such miracles Jesus sought to establish and increase the disciples' faith in his deity.

Preparation

Brainstorm people who are special to the children. In small groups write down what makes these people special. Look at the various qualities required to make someone special. Can the children think of people, past or present, who have become important for these qualities?

Draw or bring in pictures of people who are special. Make a display.

Say that Jesus is special to Christians. Find out why this is so. Use any stories from the Bible that they know to help explain this.

Look at the story of the anointing of Jesus at Bethany

(Mark 14:3–9). Ask the children why the woman might have wanted to 'waste' the perfume on Jesus.

Look at the story of the calming of the storm (Mark 4:35–41). How did the disciples react? Why might this story be important to Christians?

Practise making sound effects for the storm using musical instruments or hands and voices ie groups of children clicking fingers, rubbing hands together, clapping hands, whistling etc can gradually be built up into a crescendo.

Presentation

Leader: We all have people who are special to us for different reasons. These are some of our special people.
(*A number of children show their pictures and briefly explain why that person is special*)
Leader: Someone who is very special to Christians is Jesus. The Bible tells us about the many things he did while on earth. Here is one occasion when the disciples realised he was different.
Reader: Mark 4:35–41
The calming of the storm could be mimed while one child reads the story from the Bible. When the storm begins to blow up other members of the class can make sound effects a suggested above.
Leader: The disciples were amazed at Jesus' power. Many of the people who met Jesus thought he was special, as the following story shows.
Reader: Mark 14:3–9
Again one child can read while another group mimes.
Leader: The woman in the story thought Jesus was so special that she wanted to show him by doing something for him. Spend a few moments thinking about the people who are special to you.

Follow up

Ask the children to identify other people who can be regarded as important today. Can people be important long after they are dead? If so, in what ways?

Consider the idea that everyone is important, whether they are famous or not. Look at the assembly outline 'What am I worth?'

Think about people to whom the children are special and why? Does this give them any sense of responsibility?

21   Obeying the rules

Aim

To think about why we have rules and to look at the rules that God has given us.

Bible base

Exodus 20:1–17 The ten commandments
Mark 12:28–34 Jesus gives the great commandment

Preparation

Discuss why we have rules. Look at magazine pictures of cyclists and walkers by the river and talk about what rules apply to them.

Think about some of the laws that apply to the children, eg no riding of bicycles on the pavement, no buying of cigarettes under age 16. In pairs pick one of the laws and talk about why it exists.

Ask the children if they have heard of the Ten Commandments. Do they know any of them? Look them up in the Bible. They fall into two groups: some are about loving God, others about loving people (your neighbours). Draw two circles and label them 'Love God' and 'Love your neighbour'. Write the laws in the right group.

Write the Commandments on separate pieces of paper. Then ask groups of children to try and rank them in order of importance, drawing out the reasons for their decisions. Look at the Bible passage in Mark 12:28–34, where Jesus summarises the law into two rules. Do they cover everything in life?

Look at different words associated with rules eg laws, rules, instructions, orders, guidelines, commandments. Do they all mean the same thing? Which are stronger than others?

Brainstorm some ground rules for the classroom. Try and encourage them to be positive rather than negative eg respect someone else's property rather than don't steal, listen to each other rather than don't talk when someone else is speaking.

Display them on the wall eg in speech bubbles. Focus on one of the rules occasionally to see how well they are keeping it.

Presentation

Two children start the assembly by playing a simple game, eg noughts and crosses. As they play, one of them breaks the rules in different ways, ie having two goes, rubbing out the other player's marks etc. The second player complains and they gradually introduce rules into the game.

Reader: We have been thinking about rules in our class. We follow rules in all sorts of situations.

(*Here a number of children can demonstrate different examples of following rules, eg safety rules in the kitchen, riding a bike, crossing the road, playing another game, at the swimming pool, school rules.*)

If we don't follow the rules we can get into a mess, and possibly even into danger. In the same way that we have school rules and other rules to tell us how to behave, God gave his people some rules or commandments to tell them the best way to live.

Narrator: Moses climbed down from the top of the mountain, called Mount Sinai. He was carrying the ten rules which were God's ways. They were carved in stone. Four of the rules told people how they should love God, the others told them how to love one another.

Moses: These are the ten rules . . . (*have the Ten Commandments written out for display*)

Don't have any other gods.

Don't make any images to worship.

Don't use God's name in wrong ways.

Keep one day of the week special in order to rest and worship.

Respect your parents.

Don't murder.

Don't take anyone else's wife or husband.

Don't steal.

Don't tell lies.

Don't be greedy for things that belong to other people.

Narrator: When Jesus was on earth, he was asked about these rules, or Commandments. Let's see what he thought of them.

Teacher of the law: Which of the commands is most important?

Jesus: The most important command is this: Love the Lord your God with all your heart, with all your soul, all your mind, and with all your strength. The second most important command is this: Love your neighbour as yourself.

Narrator: Jesus shortened the rules that we looked at earlier. He said we should love God and one another. We have rules to help us not to make life miserable. Here are some of the rules we've agreed upon for our class.

(*Here the ground rules decided on earlier may be read out.*)

Follow up

Are there any extra rules needed for inside the school, or the playground? If so, why?

Let the children make up their own ten commandments. They could be funny or serious, eg ten rules for pleasing my mum or ten rules for annoying my teacher.

In *Christianity Topic Book Two* by Margaret Cooling, published by RMEP, there is a whole section on rules, for further ideas.

Section 3   Special Occasions

22   Harvest

Aim

To help the children appreciate the wonder of God's world.

Preparation

Bring in various seeds and ask the children what they grow into.

Focus on a harvest hymn, eg Lord of the Harvest. See outline 25 for further ideas on this approach.

Brainstorm things that are harvested. Broaden the discussion to include things other than crops eg fish. What things do we eat from other countries? How are they grown and harvested? What makes a good/bad harvest? What happens to surplus food?

Paint pictures of an oak tree, horse chestnut, sunflower, a gardener/farmer, a garden with nothing growing in it and the same garden full of flowers.

Presentation

Leader: This morning we're thinking about harvest. (N) is going to read to us from the Bible.
Reader: The parable of the mustard seed, Mark 4:30–32
Leader: Large things start from small beginnings. A mustard seed is very, very small and yet it can grow into a large plant.

Each of us started life as a tiny baby, but as the years have gone by we've grown taller. (*Choose children from different age groups to stand up to illustrate this*).

Jesus told this story to explain to his disciples that although only a few people would believe in him to start with, they would tell others. As more people heard about Jesus he would have more and more followers, and God's kingdom would grow. Sure enough there are now Christians all over the world. It's not only mustard seeds that grow from being very small to being very large. We're going to look at some other things.

A: What have you got there?

B: Don't you know? It's an acorn.

A: An acorn? What use is something as small as that?

B: Well, if you plant it in the ground it will grow.

A: Into a giant acorn?

B: No, into an oak tree (*shows picture*).

C: What have you got there?

D: It's a conker.

C: A conker? What do you do with it?

D: You can have conker fights with it but it's supposed to fall into the ground so that it can grow.

C: What does it grow into?

D: A horse chestnut tree (*shows picture*).

E: What have you got in that bag?

F: Sunflower seeds – they'll grow into sunflowers (*shows picture*).

G: Look what I've got! A packet of seeds.

H: What will they grow into?

G: I'm not sure, but I can plant them in my garden (*shows picture of empty garden*), and if I look after them, maybe next year I'll have a beautiful garden.

H: (*holding up picture of 'beautiful garden'*) Like this?

G: Yes, like that.

J: (*eating apple, finds pip*) What's this?

K: It's an apple pip.

J: What do you do with it?

K: Well, if you plant it in the ground, it might grow into an apple tree, then you'd have your own apples. (*Holds up picture of apple tree.*)

J: Great! I can hardly wait! Will I have apples by next year?
K: I'm afraid not. Apple trees take several years to grow.
J: Huh! I can't be bothered with that! (*throws apple down*).
(*'Growing music' plays and a child dressed as an apple tree
grows from where the apple fell.*)
K: That's amazing!

One of the children could write a prayer thanking God for
seeds, for sending rain and sunshine to help them grow and
for all the good things that grow from tiny seeds for us to eat.

Follow up

The children could take part in a tree study – identifying
them, measuring them, classifying them etc.

If there is a wooded area near the school take the children
in groups of ten. Arrange them in pairs. One child of each
pair is blindfolded. The other child leads her to a tree. The
blindfolded one is encouraged to explore the tree, feeling it
thoroughly. The pair return to the starting point. Without
the blindfold the 'blind' one must identify their tree. Swap
over.

My leaf – present the children with a box of leaves from
the same tree. Ask each child to take a leaf and examine it
closely. Leaves are returned to the box and muddled up. Each
child is then asked to pick out their leaf.

Apple study – find out the different types of apples and
where they grow? What do they look like? How much do they
cost? Which is the most popular apple in the class?

Make a large harvest collage with the sky, fields and the
sea, with a border of vegetables around the edge.

23 Famine in a world of plenty

Aim

To consider the problem of hunger in the world and what can be done about it.

Bible base

Matthew 25:35–40, The final judgement. John 6:1–14, Feeding the five thousand.

Preparation

Relief agencies such as TEAR fund, Oxfam, Christian Aid, Save The Children will be able to supply you with information and resources for the theme. Newspapers provide current examples of natural disasters, famines, floods etc. Children could write their own newspaper articles. Ask the children to write poems about famine, poverty and hunger.

Discuss what causes famine.

Look at the story of the feeding of the five thousand (John 6:1–14) and look at the boy's response to the situation.

Look at the story of the king's dream in Genesis 41 and how Joseph planned for the famine.

Look at the word 'Harvest' and see what other words the children can make using the letters. There are a lot that come out on the theme eg. share, eat, tea, earth, tears, have, heart etc.

Paint the letters of 'harvest' on individual cards.

Presentation

Use the following outline or ask children to write their own, incorporating the words they've discovered in 'Harvest'.

Leader: At this time of year we are thinking about harvest (*children hold up the letters*) when we give thanks to God for all the good things he provides on the 'earth' (*children rearrange themselves, here and where words are in quotes*) like animals, crops etc. In our country there are plenty of things for us to 'eat', but in many parts of the world people 'starve'. Two-thirds of the earth's population go hungry. If we were to 'share' our resources things would be different, there is sufficient food in our world for all. We could 'save' many people from premature death. This would prevent a great many 'tears' when people lose their loved ones due to lack of food. What should be our 'heart's' response?

(*The children could then act out the story of the feeding of the five thousand, from John 6:1–14.*)

Leader: The boy probably thought there was little he could do when there were so many people who were hungry. However he was prepared to share what he had and Jesus was able to use it.

(*Children then read out some of their poems.*)

Leader: Are we willing to use the little we have to help others?

(*Prayers written by the children.*)

Follow up

Look at imports and exports using a large map to stick on labels from various products from all over the world.

Discuss what could be done about school waste, eg dinners etc.

In famine areas what choices are open to onlookers and sufferers? Why do some people decide to help eg Bob Geldof, whilst others refuse?

Play 'The world feast game', a simulation game concerning world food production, available from Christian Aid, or the following game: 'The Great Fudge Crisis'.

Each player is given a bag of fudge pieces (or equivalent)

which represents food. The game leader has absolute authority. Arguing with her could mean forfeiting the bag of fudge and a trip to 'Never-never land.' A player needs to turn in three pieces of fudge to the game leader when she says it's the end of a day. A day lasts four minutes.

When the game leader says it's the end of a day, everyone sits down and she collects the three pieces of fudge. If a player can't give the leader three pieces he goes to 'Never-never land' for the remainder of the game.

During the four minute day, players can bargain and beg for pieces of fudge from the others. A player can share his fudge freely or require that the begging player works for his fudge by doing a simple task eg five press-ups. The game lasts 5 days (20 mins).

Before the game count out fifteen pieces of fudge for each player, but don't tell the group that there is enough food to feed everyone. (This shows that in reality there is enough food in the world but it is not distributed properly). Unevenly distribute the fudge in the bags, but give the players at least three pieces.

When the game begins the leader can declare war, hurricane, famine etc. and take pieces of fudge from whoever she wants. She can also declare good weather etc and give fudge to others. If stealing occurs the leader should inform the victim that sometimes life is unfair.

At the end of the five days gather the group together to discuss what happened. How many people died? Why? What methods were used to get the fudge? If you had more fudge than you needed, how did you feel? If you had less? How easy was it to share?

How fair was life to you during the five days? Point out that there was enough fudge for everyone to get through all five days alive.

Organise a 1p/2p/5p line, asking children to bring in coins on a certain day. Lay them around the hall or along the corridor, or stick on a map of eg Africa. Collect the money for a relief agency.

24 The four beggars

This assembly has been adapted from a story in *Plays for Assembly* by Peter M. Allen, published by Schofield and Sims Ltd.

It could be used as a follow on from the last assembly or used on its own as an assembly about sharing, to back up the story of the feeding of the five thousand.

Presentation

Narrator: There were four very foolish beggars clothed in rags, begging in a small village. All day they sat in the market place and held out their bowls begging for food or money from those who passed by.

Beggar 1: I'm so hungry, please give me something to eat.

Woman: Here's some meat for you. I hope you enjoy it.

Beggar 2: Please give me something to eat, my stomach's empty.

Man: Certainly, here are some vegetables you can have.

Beggar 3: Please give me something to eat, I haven't had anything all day.

Woman 2: All I've got are a few spices, but you're welcome to them if you like.

Beggar 4: Help me, help me. I'm starving. I shall die soon if I don't have something to eat.

Man 2: I haven't got much but you can have some rice. Will that do?

Narrator: Later that day, as the sun was setting, the four beggars met together to talk about their day.

Beggar 1: What a day! All I've got is a small piece of meat. That won't last long.

Beggar 2: All I've got are a few vegetables. That won't fill me up.

Beggar 3: All I've got are a few spices. What use are they?

Beggar 4: All I've got is a little bit of rice. That won't keep me alive for long.

Beggar 1: I know what we can do! If we put some water in the pot over the fire, we can all throw in our own bit of food and we can make a stew and there will be enough for everyone.

Beggar 2: What a good idea!

Beggar 3: Then we will be full up.

Beggar 4: Come on then. Let's get on with it.

Narrator: But the first beggar realised that if he kept his meat for himself and the other three threw in their food, he could enjoy it for himself afterwards as well as having the stew. So he pretended to drop his meat into the pot, but really he put it into his pocket for later.

The second beggar had the same idea. He did the same with his vegetables.

The third beggar did the same with his spices.

The fourth beggar did the same with his rice.

So each of the beggars had pretended to throw what they had into the pot.

Beggar 1: It will be ready now. Hold out your bowls and I fill them with delicious stew. Well, does it taste good?

Beggar 2: It's not as nice as I thought it would be.

Beggar 3: I thought it would be better than this.

Beggar 4: It doesn't taste of anything much.

Beggar: It tastes just like warm water.

Narrator: The four foolish beggars sat there eating a stew which was nothing but warm water. None of them would admit what they'd done. In trying to be greedy they had tricked one another. And they were still hungry!

25 Autumn days

An assembly based on the song 'Autumn days when the grass is jewelled' found in *Come and Praise* (BBC).

Aim

To encourage the children to look at the beauty of autumn.

Preparation

Children often bring in berries, fruits etc. Use these to introduce the theme of autumn.

Pictures could be painted to illustrate each line of each verse. Children who present each line should prepare a few sentences about it.

eg 1 'Autumn days when the grass is jewelled'
When I walk to school on Autumn mornings, the grass verges are all wet. Water droplets sparkle in the sun and it looks as if the grass is covered with diamonds.

eg 2 'and the silk inside a chestnut shell'
Conkers. Prickly green cases lying on the ground.
They all seem to be empty; not a conker to be found.
But as I look more carefully, beneath the conker tree
I see it buried in the grass – a conker that's for me.
It is no longer tucked away inside a covering shell,
Smooth inside a prickly coat – oh yes I know it well.
I'll show it to my brother; we'll have a conker fight.
With a conker that's as big as this I'm sure to do alright.

Presentation

The class sings the whole song through once. Two or three children should then read out poems they have written about autumn.

Verse 1 should be sung again, before the pictures and poems for that verse are presented.

The chorus and verse 2 should be sung, then children present pictures and words for that verse. This should be repeated for verses 3 and 4. After verse 4 has been illustrated, the chorus can be sung.

Children can read prayers that they have written to thank God for the things that they like about autumn.

The whole school can sing the song together as children show their pictures again.

26 Christmas

Aim

To help the children think about the true meaning of Christmas.

Bible base

Luke 2:1–20; Matthew 1:18, 2:12. The birth of Jesus.

Preparation

The children will already be well into thinking about Christmas by the time you come to prepare this assembly so it is good to remind them that the reason for the festival is because a special baby was born – God's son.

As an introduction you could ask the children to write down what Christmas means to them and compare answers.

They could look up and read the story for themselves in the Bible.

They could write a modern day version of the story. Where would Jesus be born today? What would the papers say? Imagine you were Mary's best friend – how might you have felt? Look at Christmas traditions around the world.

Presentation

Participants: carol singers, party-goers, photographer and photographer's wife, Mary, Joseph, 3 shepherds, 3 kings, woodman and family, bishop, Santa, soloist and narrator.

100

Smile Please!

The following play is written in a pantomime style in order to produce an impact at the final stage when the point is made.

The play incorporates a number of traditions from different countries which could be left out or others added accordingly. *(On stage are carol singers and party-goers already in position for the photograph. A lot of fuss and noise is being made.*

Carol Singers: *Sing 'Jingle Bells', pull crackers and throw streamers. Jokes are read out.)*

Party goer 1: Here, listen to this. What do you get if you eat Christmas decorations?

PG 2: I don't know. What do you get if you eat Christmas decorations?

PG 1: Tinselitus

PG 3: How about this one. Why is it difficult to keep a secret in the North Pole?

PG 4: I don't know, why is it difficult to keep a secret in the North Pole?

PG 3: Your teeth tend to chatter!

(The children will know plenty of other jokes that could be added here . . .)

Carol Singers: Jingle Bells . . .

Photographer: All right! All right! Calm down will you. I know you're excited but I've got a difficult job to do. I've got important people coming from all over the world so that I can take a photograph of Christmas. Now just wait quietly, please.

Enter Mary and Joseph. Greeted by photographer's wife. Mary and Joseph take seats.

Wife: I'll just fetch the crib for you

Mary: Thank you. It's nice and warm in here, much cosier than the stable we had.

Photographer: Hello there. Have you seen anyone else on your travels?

Joseph: Yes, we met some German Shepherds a while back.

Photographer: Oh no not again! I'll have to phone the dog catcher first thing in the morning.

101

Song: Stille Nacht . . .

Enter 3 Shepherds

Photog: Come in, come in. We've been expecting you.

Hans: Hello, my name is Hans.

Bumpsa: Hello, my name is Bumpsa.

Neece: Hello, my name is Neece.

Enter wife with crib

Photog: Ah, I'd like you to meet my wife Daisy. Hans, Neece and Bumpsa, Daisy. Find a space quickly, will you, because I think the wise men are on their way.

Enter three Kings

King 1: We are the three kings. We have come from the east.

Photog: We thought you would have been here earlier.

King 2: Our train was late.

Wife: Oh, Kings Cross?

King 3: Yes, King's very cross. We make complaint.

Wife: Oh well . . . go and find a space and do try to smile.

Photographer looks through camera at scene

Wife: Hold on, who's this strange fella coming?

Photog: That's not a fella, it's a woman.

Enter Woodman

Photog: Excuse me, but who are you?

Woodman: I'm a woodman.

Wife: See, I told you he was a fella. Get it? Woodman, fella!

Photog: Well, what have you got to do with Christmas?

Woodman: In Germany I am very famous because one Christmas Eve my family looked after a small boy who turned out to be the Christ Child.

Photog: Oh and is your family with you?

Woodman: Yes and we have brought a Christmas tree for your picture.

Enter family.

Wife: I don't like to worry you, but there's a Bishop coming.

Photog: What! A real one?

Enter Bishop

Photog: Er, hello your vicarship. I er, don't appear to have you on my list.

Bishop: I am Nicholas. I have come from Holland. At Christmas time I give presents to all children who are good.

Photog: Oh right. Well, come and join the picture.
(*Photog. goes to camera and looks through*)
Yes, that's looking good. I don't think we've got room for many more.
Wife: I shouldn't be so sure. I think I can see reindeer.
Photog: Oh no, and we've left the washing out as well.
Wife: No I mean Rudolph and his friends. They're pulling Father Christmas.
Enter reindeer, Father Christmas and helpers.
Santa: Ho, ho, ho! Merry Christmas everybody. I hope you don't mind but I've brought my helpers along too.
Wife: No not at all, the more the merrier.
Photog: Now look at the camera and smile please. No wait a minute, it's not quite right.
Santa is moved from left to right but photographer is still not happy. After a lot of thought he says
Photog: I'm afraid this will just have to go.
Mary, Joseph and the crib are moved out of the picture and Santa sits right in the middle. He looks through the camera.
Ah that's much better, now smile please.
As photograph is taken a baby is heard crying off stage.
Solo: Once in Royal David's City (*or something similar*)
Narrator: This Christmas as we enjoy parties, presents and all the fun that goes on, let us not be like the photographer and miss the real meaning of Christmas.

Follow up

You could make a large collage with a stable scene at the centre and all the 'trappings' around the edge.

27 The sad Christmas cracker

Aim

To remind the children about why we celebrate Christmas.

Bible base

Luke 2:1–20. Matthew 1:18–2:12. The Christmas story.

Preparation

The previous outline suggests some activities which would be appropriate here.

Talk to the children about how they prepare for Christmas. This will introduce them to the theme of decorations.

Look at the story. It could be presented either by the children acting out the various parts or by preparing simple card puppets and using props.

Presentation

Narrator: It was Christmas Eve and the Smith family were making final preparations for the following day.

(Here the family finish putting up decorations, placing presents under the tree etc.)

Eventually everything was ready and in spite of the protests of the children the Smiths headed off to bed. But as they disappeared upstairs everything was not as it should be in the room they left.

Christmas tree: I'm glad they have gone. My arms are aching terribly with all the baubles and chocolates they keep adding on. All my needles are falling off in this heat as well. I can't wait to get back to the garden.

Christmas lights: You think you've been working hard! All we've done all day is switch on, off, on, off. We're exhausted!

Tinsel: You lot are always complaining. I'm having a marvellous time, gently glittering and cheering the place up no end.

Angel (*from the top of the tree*): Yes, come on, everyone, it's worth all the trouble. Think of all the fun we'll have tomorrow.

Lights: Hang on a minute! What's that noise? We can hear someone crying.

Narrator: As they listened carefully the Christmas cracker could be heard sobbing at the bottom of the tree.

Tinsel: Whatever's the matter?

Cracker: Well it's OK for all of you. You'll all be back next year. But not me! Oh no. What'll have happened to me? I'll have been pulled apart!

Angel: But you've no reason to be sad. You have a very important job to do tomorrow.

Cracker: And what might that be?

Angel: Well you help us remember different parts of the Christmas story. Let's see.

(*Here two children demonstrate with a cracker*)

Angel: The bang reminds us of the surprise the shepherds received when the angels came and told them about the birth of Jesus.

(*A tableau of the shepherds being visited by the angels could be presented*)

Angel: And what do you have inside? Well there's a little present. That helps to remind us of the gifts the wise men brought to the baby Jesus. Gifts of gold, frankincense, and myrrh. It also shows us that God gave Jesus to the world as a present.

(*Again a tableau of the wise men visiting Jesus could be shown*)

Angel: There's also a paper hat – it's in the shape of a crown. From this we remember that the baby Jesus was a special kind of king.

Cracker: I'm feeling better already!

Angel: Ah, but I haven't finished yet. There's also a message or motto on a piece of paper. That first Christmas, God gave us a special motto. Another name given to Jesus was Immanuel and it means God is with us. So you see, you really are very important.

Cracker: I understand now. I'm really looking forward to tomorrow.

Narrator: So when you pull your crackers this year remember the surprise of the shepherds. When you find your gift, think of the presents of the wise men and the gift God has given to us. As you put on your paper crown be reminded that Jesus was a special king. And when you read your motto, remember that Christmas is about God being with us.

Follow up

Look at other Christmas customs.

Get the children to write about their Christmas day from the point of view of the Christmas tree, a present etc.

Let the children imagine that they are one of the people around at the time of Jesus' birth, eg a shepherd, innkeeper or wise man and ask them to write the story from this point of view.

28   Lent 1 – Jesus in the wilderness

A series of two assemblies looking at the theme of temptation and how Jesus reacted to temptation.

Aim

To explain how Christians remember the temptation of Jesus in the wilderness during the time of Lent.

Bible base

Matthew 4:1–11; Luke 4:1–13. The temptation of Jesus.

Preparation

Look up and read the story of Jesus in the wilderness. What did Jesus do when he was tempted? What gave him the power to resist?

Look at the traditions associated with Shrove Tuesday and Ash Wednesday. Explain that Ash Wednesday marks the beginning of Lent in which individuals try to approach Good Friday in a serious frame of mind. The forty days of fasting which occur in Lent (Sundays do not count as fast days) are a reminder of Jesus' time in the wilderness.

Presentation

This assembly should be done on or near to Ash Wednesday.

Leader: Ash Wednesday marks the beginning of Lent. It is a time when Christians think carefully about themselves as they prepare for Easter. (*Some children could give further* *details about Ash Wednesday, as found in the Living Festivals Omnibus* RMEP). The forty days of Lent also remind us of the days when Jesus was tempted in the wilderness and how he overcame it. Watch what happened during that time.

The poem can be mimed by one group and read by a narrator, devil and Jesus.

Into the desert went Jesus alone,
His bed was a sand dune, his pillow a stone.
He thought and he prayed, had nothing to eat,
When up came the devil, who sensed his defeat.

'I know you are hungry, your tummy must ache,
So turn this flat stone into a rock cake!
There's really no problem, to one such as you,
Imagine a sandwich, or perhaps you'd like two?'

But Jesus remembered the words he had learned,
And so to the Bible he quickly returned –
And quoted a passage, as he sat on a stone.
'Man just cannot live on bread all alone.'

The devil just sighed, and tried once again,
And flew up quite high, as if on a plane.
'Just look at those countries. Do you fancy the view?
Just worship me, and I'll give them to you.'

Into the book Jesus dipped yet once more.
'You must worship the Lord, for that is the Law.'

Jerusalem city was next on the list,
On the roof of the Temple. 'Now I insist,
Throw yourself over, it soon gets a crowd
And angels will catch you safe on a cloud.'

Jesus said firmly, to this voice in his ear,
'You've had your say now please disappear.
You've tempted me often, now I want a rest,
Do not put the Lord your God to the test.'

All these things happened, quite long ago,
But people don't change much, I'm certain you know,
That often we're tempted by a voice from within.
It's all right to be tempted, but wrong to give in.

Leader: Jesus was very strong and didn't give in. Next week we'll be thinking about some of the situations where we can ask for God's help to be strong and not give in to temptation.

Follow up

Look at effects of advertising and the influence of the media on our decision making. Make a collage of advertisements.

Make up some TV commercials based on the temptation of Jesus eg 'You look tired and hungry: you need . . .'

Read to older pupils excerpts from 'The Screwtape letters' by C. S. Lewis.

The following assembly looks into the theme of temptation in much more depth.

29   Lent 2 – Tempting situations

Aim:

To help the children to think about the issue of temptation.

Bible base:

Matthew 4:1–11. Luke 4:1–13. The temptation of Jesus.

Preparation

This is a difficult theme to tackle with children but you might like to introduce the idea with a game of Scruples. Divide the class into three groups. For each question the groups choose one person to represent them. A sample question could be, 'You find £10 in the playground, do you keep it?' Each question is asked of the panel, but in each case a different group member is asked not to answer aloud but to choose a YES/ NO card which is hidden from everyone else. Then the other two, having said what they would do, have to guess what the other person would do. One point is given for each correct guess.

Have a discussion on the meaning of temptation. How do we make judgements on what is right or wrong. What does it mean to be tempted? Is it wrong to be tempted? Do you always have a choice? What have you been tempted to do? Is it easier to make a wrong choice?

How can we combat temptation? Does it help to consider that others might get hurt or upset?

Presentation

Leader: Last week we were thinking about Jesus in the wilderness, showing how he was tempted and what his reaction was. In our class we have been thinking about some of the situations we might find ourselves in, where we could be tempted to do the wrong thing.

(The following poems could be read by one group of children and mimed at the same time by another group of children).

[DINNER TICKETS]
I was out in the playground watching this kid,
Down past the French shed, there's a real great skid,
He was sliding and shouting, went like a rocket,
When I saw this paper fall out of his pocket.
He never noticed it, but I marked the spot,
And after the whistle, look what I got,
Five dinner tickets, worth over four quid,
So I've made a profit, thanks to that kid.

[GOLD PEN]
I sat in the library, it was break and was cold,
I noticed a pen which appeared to be gold.
There was no one about, it seemed quite a shame,
I looked at it hard, but there wasn't a name.
I don't really know how, not much I don't,
It fell in my bag. I should tell, but I won't,
My Berol is knackered, I've run out of ink,
This'll do nicely, so what do you think?

[CASH FIND]
I was down by the market, you know where I mean,
I saw this old geezer get off his machine,
The oldest two wheels that you've ever seen,
He looked about ninety, and wasn't too clean.
He pulled out a hanky, and with it a note,
It looked like a tenner, the silly old goat.
I grabbed it and ran as quick as I could,
He didn't notice, never thought that he would.

[BULLY]

Once there were two of us, Kevin and me,
Chatting about soccer, under this tree.
This kid kicked a ball, it fell at our feet,
I said to Kevin, 'Let's give him a treat.'
I threw the ball, high in the air.
The kid asked politely, 'Please give it here.'
We laughed in his face and I kicked his shin,
Then Kevin ran over and put his boot in.

Leader: It's not always easy to do the right thing. Stop and think what you would have done in those situations? Why don't you talk about what you would do when you go back to your own classrooms.

Follow up

In pairs the children think up situations where a friend tries to persuade them to do something they believe is wrong. In small groups role play those situations trying to generate strategies for coping with temptation.

30 Noisy Norman

Aim

To show the children that Lent is a reflective time, and to encourage them to stop and think.

Preparation

Ask the children to list or make a pie chart of all the different ways they spend their time during a week. Look at how much time they spend quietly on their own.

Presentation

Participants: Narrators, Noisy Norman, Mr Bun, Mrs Chubb, Mr Mince (plus other shopkeepers and customers if needed), a friend, children to do sound effects.

Narrator 1: In our assembly we are visiting Quietland. Who can tell me who lives there?

Narrator 2: Of course Quietland is probably the worst place on earth for Noisy Norman to live. I don't know how well you know Noisy Norman but he could never do anything in a quiet manner.

Narrator 1: He couldn't knock on a door quietly.

Narrator 2: He couldn't drink quietly.

N1: He couldn't eat quietly.

N2: He certainly couldn't talk on the phone quietly.

N1: Now the people of Quietland were used to Noisy Norman. Let us show you a typical day in Quietland. . . .

N2: Noisy Norman was going to the shops. He went out of his house (*door bangs*). He walked down the street. (*drum* *beat*) The first shop he came to was the Post Office. He opened the door (*door opens*). He closed the door (*door closes with a bang*). He went up to the counter and said . . .

Noisy N: I WANT TO BUY A STAMP!

N2: He got his stamp and left Mrs Chubb at the Post Office trembling as he went out. (*Door bangs*)

N1: Next he went to the bakers. He opened the door (*door opens*). He closed the door (*door closes with bang*). He went up to the counter and said . . .

Noisy N: I WANT TO BUY A LOAF OF BREAD!

N1: He got his bread and left Mr. Bun the Baker trembling as he went out. (*Door bangs*)

N2: Next he went to the butchers. He opened the door (*door opens*). He closed the door (*door bangs*). He went up to the counter and said . . .

Noisy N: I WANT TO BUY SOME MEAT!

N2: Mr Mince the butcher was trembling as Noisy Norman left the shop with his meat. (*Door bangs*).

N1: Now this went on day after day. So Mrs Chubb at the Post Office, Mr Bun the baker and Mr Mince the Butcher got together and decided on a plan to stop Noisy Norman shouting.

N2: The next day Noisy Norman left home as usual (*door bangs*). He went into the Post Office (*door opens*) and closed the door (*door bangs*). He went up to the counter and said . . .

Noisy N: I WANT TO BUY A STAMP

Mrs C: Pardon? (*x3*)

N2: Eventually Noisy Norman gave up and left the Post Office (*door bangs*).

N1: Then he went into the bakers (*door opens*) and closed the door (*door bangs*). He went up to the counter and said . . .

Noisy N: I WANT TO BUY A LOAF OF BREAD!

Mr Bun: Pardon? (*x3*)

N1: Eventually Noisy Norman gave up and left the bakers (*door bangs*).

N2: Then he went into the butchers (*door opens*) and closed the door (*door bangs*). He went up to the counter and said . . .

Noisy N: I WANT TO BUY SOME MEAT!

Mr M: Pardon? (*x3*)

N2: Eventually Noisy Norman gave up and left the butchers (*door bangs*). So that day Noisy Norman went home without any of the things he needed.

N1: The next day Noisy Norman left home as usual (*door bangs*). He went into the Post Office (*door opens and bangs*). He went up to the counter and said . . .

Noisy N: I WANT TO BUY A STAMP!

Mrs C: Pardon?

Noisy N: I WANT TO BUY . . .

N1: And then he stopped . . . and then he thought . . . and then he thought again very hard . . . and then he said . . .

Noisy N: I'D LIKE TO BUY A STAMP PLEASE!

N1: Noisy Norman had never spoken that way before.

N2: Next he went into the Bakers (*door opens and bangs*). He went up to the counter and said . . .

Noisy N: I WANT TO BUY A LOAF OF BREAD

Mr B: Pardon?

Noisy N: I WANT TO BUY. . . .

N2: And then he stopped . . . and then he thought . . . and thought again very hard . . . and then he said . . .

Noisy N: I'd like to buy a loaf of bread please.

N1: Next he went into the butchers (*door opens and closes*). He went up to the counter and said:

Noisy N: I WANT TO BUY SOME MEAT!

Mr M: Pardon?

Noisy N: I WANT TO BUY. . . .

N1: And then he stopped. . . . and then he thought. . . . and he thought again very hard. . . . and then he said . . .

Noisy N: I'd like to buy some meat please.

N2: As he was walking home Noisy Norman stopped and sat down on the park bench. He stopped to think about the day he'd had. He realised that he didn't need to go around shouting in order to be heard. By taking a moment to stop and think he had realised this.

N1: On the way back to his house, someone he knew called to him . . .

Friend: Oi! Noisy Norman! How are you today?

N1: Noisy Norman turned to reply . . .

Noisy N: '. . . . ' (*opens his mouth but doesn't say anything*).

N1: and then he went home.

N2: Lent is a time when we can stop and think, whether

it's about giving up jelly babies or something a bit more important. There are many times when we rush into things without thinking and find ourselves in trouble. When Jesus was in the wilderness and throughout his life Jesus did not rush in but he stopped and thought about what God wanted him to do.

This drama is based on an idea from the *Mr Men* series by Roger Hargreaves.

Follow up

Talk about things that the children do that they regret afterwards and why they do them.

Explain the traffic light strategy. When the children get into situations where they are angry, upset etc. teach them to say to themselves Red (which means stop), then Amber (pause to think about alternative ways of reacting) then Green (try it).

31 An Easter play

Aim

To give a brief background to the events of Easter.

Bible base

Luke 19:28–40; 22:14–23, 31–34, Luke 22:39–24:12, John 20:1–18. The Easter story.

Preparation

Tell the story of the last week of Jesus' life as mentioned in the play.

Further ideas can be found in the following assembly outline.

Presentation

Leader: What does Easter mean to you? Chocolate eggs and a holiday from school? We want to show you why it is such an important time for Christians. . . .

Mother: Come on children, don't give up, we're almost there.

Reuben: Are we really? Jerusalem is much bigger than I thought it would be. It's so crowded and noisy.

Father: Jerusalem is very busy this week because the Jewish people have come to celebrate the Passover Festival.

Sarah: Why do we celebrate it, Father?

Father: We celebrate Passover to remind ourselves of how God delivered his people from slavery in Egypt hundreds of years ago.

Mother: Look at the crowd of people coming our way.

Reuben: There's a man on a donkey and the people are waving branches . . .

(*A song could be sung here*)

Reuben: Who is that man?

Sarah: Why is everyone singing and shouting?

Father: I think that is Jesus. The people are excited because they are so pleased to see him.

Mother: Some people believe he is God's promised Messiah who has come to save them.

Reuben: So that's why everyone is so happy.

Father: Yes, but there are men here in Jerusalem who hate Jesus and are jealous of him because he is so popular. I am afraid for his safety. I think there might be trouble brewing.

(*Music*)

Narrator: When they arrived in Jerusalem, Jesus told Peter and John to go and get the Passover meal ready. They met together to share the Passover meal. While they were all together Jesus explained that he was soon going to die.

Jesus: This is my body which is given for you. This is my blood which is poured out for you. This is the last time you will share this meal with me because I am going to die soon.

Peter: No, master! That will never happen to you.

Jesus: I tell you, Peter; before the cock crows tonight you will say three times that you never knew me.

Peter: No Master, I would never do that. I am ready to go to prison with you, I would even die with you.

Disciple 1: Yes, so would I.

Disciple 2: I'll always stay with you, master.

Disciple 3: We will never leave you, Jesus.

Narrator: But these words were quickly forgotten. Jesus took three of his disciples with him to a quiet garden to pray. Jesus prayed to God, but the disciples were so tired they fell asleep.

Jesus: Couldn't you stay awake with me for a short while to pray?

John: We must have fallen asleep.

118

Peter: Sorry, master. Wake up, James.

James: I'm really tired tonight. I can't seem to stay awake.

Narrator: Just then some soldiers appeared in the garden and they arrested Jesus. The disciples were so frightened that they ran away. Jesus was taken to the High Priest's house. Peter followed at a safe distance and sat down by the fire in the courtyard of the house. There were a lot of people around and several recognised Peter.

Servant girl: I've seen you before. You're a friend of Jesus.

Peter: I am not, I've never seen him before.

Man: I remember seeing you with Jesus.

Peter: No, I wasn't. I don't know what you mean.

Man: This man was with Jesus. I know he was, he even speaks like him.

Peter: Look, I keep telling you, I don't know him. I've never seen him before. Just leave me alone.

Narrator: Just then there was the sound of a cock crowing in the distance. At that moment Jesus turned and looked straight at Peter. Peter remembered what Jesus had said. He was so upset he just sat down and cried.

(*Music*)

Narrator: Soon after this, Jesus was taken to the Roman Govenor, Pontius Pilate. Pilate talked to Jesus and asked him questions but Jesus hardly said a word. Pilate wanted to let Jesus go free but the people wanted him killed.

Crowd: Crucify him!

Pilate: Why? What has he done wrong?

Crowd: Crucify him!

Pilate: You do what you want with him but I'm having nothing to do with it. Bring me a bowl of water, I wash my hands of him.

Narrator: The soldiers put a purple robe on him and a crown of thorns on his head. All the people made fun of him.

Crowd: Long live the king of the Jews!

Narrator: Then Jesus was taken away and crucified.

(*Music*)

Narrator: Early on Sunday morning while it was still quite dark, Mary went to the tomb where Jesus had been laid. She saw that the stone had been rolled away from the entrance. She went running back to tell Peter and John.

Mary: Jesus has gone! His body isn't there any more. It must have been taken away. Where could it be?

Narrator: Peter and John followed her to the tomb and were amazed at what they saw. They rushed off to tell the other disciples, but Mary stood crying outside the tomb. Someone spoke to her. She thought it must be the gardener.

Jesus: Why are you crying? Who are you looking for?

Mary: Please, sir, if you have taken my Lord away, tell me where you have taken him so that I might go to him.

Jesus: Mary!

Mary: Oh master, it's you! You're alive!

Jesus: Yes, Mary. It's true. Go and tell my disciples that I am alive.

Mary: Listen everyone! Jesus is alive, I've seen him.

Disciples (*turning to each other*): That's wonderful! Jesus is alive!

Follow up

Read the resurrection accounts from all four gospels, Matthew 28, Mark 16, Luke 24, John 20, 21. Discuss variations in the Gospel accounts of the empty tomb. Discuss reporting events from different angles, eg sporting events and how reports can differ. What facts do all accounts clearly agree on?

Look at the traditions of Easter. Find out how they originated and where they fit into the story (if they do!).

32   Easter – On the way to the cross

Aim

To present the facts of Good Friday by focusing on the people Jesus would have met on his way to the cross.

Bible base

John 18:28 – 19:30. Matthew 27:11–56. Mark 14:43–65 and 15:1–41. Luke 23:1–49. The Crucifixion.

Crucifixion was used by the Romans to execute criminals and it was a particularly cruel and lingering death. The beating before it was also very painful as the whip would have had little pieces of lead on the thongs.

The several trials which Jesus was subjected to were because there was really no charge against him. The Jews thought he was guilty of blasphemy, ie of claiming to be God, but this was not a crime in Roman law so the charge of claiming to be king was trumped up.

It is important to look at the resurrection because it substantiates Jesus' claim that he was God.

Preparation

Read the story of Jesus' death and resurrection from the Bible or ask the children to look up the various accounts. You could also show one of the Scripture Union videos recommended in the resources listed at the end of the book.

Talk about how our faces reflect feelings and how we communicate non verbally.

Explain that as Jesus would have made his way to the cross

121

along the Via Dolorosa in Jerusalem (Luke 23:26–33) many people would have gathered to watch. They would have shown many different emotions – hate, worry, love etc.

The children could choose a character who might have been present and then make a mask (using paper plates, paper bags or papier mache) depicting their feelings. Discuss how they would have felt and what emotions would be shown on their faces. Obviously the more background the children have the better. Some examples are as follows:–

A pharise: a Jew who was dedicated to keeping the Jewish law. They disliked Jesus because he often challenged what they said and did.

A money changer: they set up their stall in the temple to take advantage of worshippers who had to give money in the local currency. Earlier in the week Jesus had thrown them out (Matthew 21:12–13)

A lawyer: teachers of the Law had been trying to trick Jesus and to find a way of getting rid of him (Luke 22:1–2).

Someone who had been healed by Jesus.

A Roman soldier: their job was to keep order and to guard prisoners. They would have been in charge of the details of the execution.

A child who had been there on Palm Sunday.

A disciple, eg Peter.

Someone in the crowd who'd never heard of Jesus.

A woman follower, eg Mary.

When the children have made their masks, help them to think through how their character would walk, how they'd respond to other characters, what they would say to Jesus as he walked past etc.

Presentation

Leader: Easter is a special time for Christians. It is just as important as Christmas but in a different way. At Easter we remember that Jesus died. Listen while we read you some of the story.

Reading: Mark 15:1–15 or John 18:28 – 19:16 or summarise in your own words the story of Jesus' arrest and trial.

Leader: As Jesus was led to the hill where he was to be

crucified many people gathered to watch.

(Mark out a pathway on the floor using masking tape. One child takes the part of Jesus and staggers along the path, the others wearing their masks call out their responses.)

Reading: John 19:17–30

Leader: All this happened on the first Good Friday, but that isn't the end of the story. The Bible goes on to say that three days later, on the first Easter day, Jesus came alive again, showing that he is the son of God.

(The children could make further masks of how the disciples felt after the resurrection).

Follow up

Look up the resurrection stories in Luke 24:13–52 and John 20:1 – 21:24.

Children may want to spend time talking about the injustice in the story. Ask the children what their feelings about such a death would have been. Was there a reason or was it just a waste? Explain that his followers saw his death as the end of everything – a tragic mistake; but when he came back they saw there was a purpose to it. Read Philippians 2:6–11. What does the writer see as the reason behind Jesus' death?

Build up a sound picture of what it might have been like at the foot of the cross. Different groups represent different people eg the soldiers, the disciples, the angry crowd, imagining a phrase they might have said. The different groups are cued in, ending with one soldier saying, 'Surely he was the Son of God'. It is very effective if taped.

33   Whitsun – Open heart surgery

Aim

To look at the Fruit of the Spirit

Bible base

Galatians 5:22–26. 1 Corinthians 13:4–7. Fruit of the Spirit.

This assembly is about what Christians call the 'fruit of the Spirit'. It can be used at any time of the year but you might like to use it during Whitsun or Pentecost when the coming of the Holy Spirit is celebrated. Christians believe that it is God at work in their lives (the Holy Spirit) which helps them to produce this fruit.

Preparation

Read the Bible passages and talk about examples of how these virtues are shown. In groups make up little plays where someone is being kind etc.

Presentation

Leader: Good morning, everyone! This morning we welcome you into the home of Shane and Tracey Jovart. They are arguing. Let's listen in on their latest argument.

TJ: The trouble with you, Shane, is that you're greedy . . . yes, that's what you are . . . just plain greedy.

SJ: Yes, dear. Are there any more cakes?

Greed: Oh good, Mrs Greed. I've managed to work my way into his heart. It took a long time but at last I've done it.

Mrs Greed: Well done Mr Greed (*They dance joyfully*)

TJ: And another thing, Shane . . . you're selfish. The only person you ever think about is yourself. Self! Self! Self! That's all you ever think about.

SJ: Yes, dear.

Mrs Selfishness: I don't believe it, Mr Selfishness! It's wonderful. There are very few people who are totally 100% selfish, but Shane is obviously one of them.

Selfishness: Great stuff, Mrs Selfishness!

TJ: And you're so impatient, Shane. You can never wait for anything. It always has to be done when you want it.

SJ: You're quite right dear, NOW WHERE'S MY TEA?!

Impatience: Well done, Shane. I can't wait to see you become even more impatient. I just can't wait! Can you, Mrs Impatience?

Mrs Impatience: No, I can't, Mr Impatience.

TJ: Whilst we're talking about your faults, I think it's true to say that you don't always tell the truth, Shane.

SJ: Yes I do, Tracey.

TJ: Really, Shane? Where were you last night?

SJ: Oh . . . er . . . I was visiting Uncle Fred.

TJ: But he died two years ago.

SJ: Oh yes, I forgot.

Dishonesty: He told a lie, Mrs Dishonesty. He told a lie!

Mrs D: Things can only get better from now on! Yippee!

TJ: But the thing that really annoys me most of all is that you never smile. You're so miserable.

SJ: What is there to smile about when you are always moaning at me?

Mrs Misery: That's right, Shane, you tell her. And don't, whatever you do, don't you dare give in and look cheerful.

Mr Misery: You know you're happiest when you're miserable.

TJ: I think what you really need to change you into a good citizen is a change of heart. I'm going to phone the hospital now.

(*Phones hospital. Four ambulance people turn up, take a limb each and carry SJ to hospital. Put on table.*)

Receptionist: Good morning, sir. Could I take a few details before your operation please? Name?

SJ: Shane Jovart.

Receptionist: And what operation are you having?

SJ: Change of heart.

Receptionist: I see. Thank you.

(*Enter surgeon and doctors/nurses*)

Surgeon: Right, young man. I've studied your notes and it seems to me that the only course of action is open heart surgery. You really need a complete change of heart and I think surgery is the only answer. Are we ready, team?

Nurse: Ready when you are sir!

Surgeon: Scalpel (scalpel), knife (knife), scissors (scissors), clamp (clamp), blindfold (blindfold? What for?) I can't stand the sight of blood. Now let's see what we've got. (*Pulls out papers one by one*)

Greed? No we don't want that. Selfishness? That can go. Dishonesty? There's no room for that. Impatience? No time for that. Misery? That'll never do. (*Characters fall down as mentioned*).

Now check the cavity will you, nurse?

Nurse 1: There are no more bad things in there, sir.

Nurse 2: But there's an awfully big hole! How are you going to fill it?

Surgeon: Ah good question, nurse. And I happen to have the answer. We're going to fill his heart with good things. Kindness (kindness), love (love), joy (joy), honesty (honesty), patience (patience)

Doctor: Shall I fill his heart with all these good things sir?

Surgeon: Of course. There's plenty of room for them all.

Kindness: I've been trying to get into Shane's heart for a long time – I'm so pleased he's found space for me at last. (*Gives paper to doctor*).

Honesty: Well, I'll be honest with you, I never thought I'd work my way into Shane's heart. This is a wonderful day.

Joy: I'm absolutely delighted that Shane has allowed me into his heart. This calls for a celebration.

Patience: I was prepared to wait for as long as it took to take my place in Shane's heart. I'm really pleased it's happened so quickly.

Surgeon: Right. That seems to have filled the hole nicely. Stitch him up please, nurse.

Nurse: Certainly, sir.

Doctor: And now for the final bandages. These are provided by love.

Love: (*As Shane is being bandaged*) Love is patient and kind; it is not jealous or conceited or proud. Love is not selfish or ill-mannered or irritable. Love is not happy with evil but is happy with the truth. Love never gives up and its faith, hope and patience never fail. Love is eternal.

Surgeon: Well, Shane, we've done all we can for you now. It's up to you to go home and really make this new heart work for you.

SJ: Oh I will, doctor, I will.

TJ: Yes, doctor, I'll make sure of that. (*Exit*)

Narrator: A few weeks later we called back to visit Shane and Tracey to see how Shane was getting on. This is what we heard.

TJ: Do you know, Shane, you're a different person since you spent that time in hospital. Life has been so much better since then. I really like your change of heart, Shane Jovart!

Follow up

Make a fruit collage (in a basket, on a tree, on a market stall). Ask for suggestions of different 'virtues' to go on them.

Give a group of children one of the bad habits that Shane first exhibited eg. greed and get them to make a monster with their bodies to represent that habit. The monster can't speak but it can make noises. Others can guess which one they've been given. In the same groups children could make up short snappy adverts for something that represents the opposite 'fruit'.

34   The Bible – a special book

Aim

To show that the Bible is a special book.

Bible Base

2 Kings 22 and 23. King Josiah discovers the book of Law.

Preparation

Talk about all the different types of books available, eg novels, manuals, dictionaries, catalogues.

Which are the children's favourite books? Which books are more important or influential than others?

Introduce the Bible as a special book. Find out how it was put together and how it is used today. (Useful books are *How the Bible came to us*: Meryl Doney, published by Lion and *Look into the Bible* published by Scripture Union)

Look at the story in 2 Kings where Josiah finds part of the Bible, the book of the Law. Show them where Deuteronomy is in the Bible. Why was it an important discovery?

Make four flash cards- 'The book was lost' with a face on a book looking sad; 'The book was found' with a happy face; 'The book was read' with a face with glasses; 'The book was obeyed' a book with legs running.

Make scrolls, using paper and dowelling rods.

A Book Lost

A Book Found

A Book Read

A Book Obeyed

Presentation

Leader: We have been looking at some of the books which are important to us.

(*Some of the children show their 'important book' and explain why it is important.*)

Leader: The Bible is an important book, made up of many books which were written over many years. People haven't always taken notice of it and for a while part of the Bible was lost. This is the story.

Narrator: The story begins with King Manasseh, who was king of Israel 700 years before Christ. He was king for fifty-five years. He took no notice of God, he worshipped the stars, he practised magic and he even sacrificed one of his own sons. When he died, his son Amon became king, but he was just as bad as his father. Part of the problem was that a book had been lost. The lost book was part of the Bible called the book of the law, which told people how to live. It was written on a scroll (*show one of the children's*). This scroll had been lost and people forgot what it said.

Narrator 2: Josiah was only eight when he became king. Imagine being a king at that age! He was a good king, unlike his father and grandfather and he followed God. He decided things had to change. The Temple of the Lord was in a terrible mess. It needed repairing as well as a good spring clean. Josiah sent for the High Priest.

Josiah: Get a wooden chest and put it outside the temple door. Then let everyone know we want money to repair and clean up the temple.

Narrator 1: It worked. Soon there was enough money to begin. There was cleaning and polishing and banging and sawing. What a noise! So many different people were hard at work – carpenters, stone-masons, builders, painters, cleaners, sweepers and polishers.

(*Rubbish could have been scattered around beforehand and now a number of children could act out the cleaning and building etc.*)

Narrator: One day one of the builders came to the High Priest with an old box. It must have been hidden hundreds of years before, there was so much dust on it!

High Priest: What have we here? (*He pulls out a scroll and blows off the dust. Talcum powder is a good substitute!*)

Narrator: When the High Priest opened the scroll and started to read it, he realised what an important book it was. They had found part of the Bible which had been hidden away for years and years! It had been lost and now they had found it.

Narrator 2: When King Josiah heard about it, he was happy *and* sad.

Josiah: No-one has been reading God's special book and obeying all his laws. It's not enough to rebuild the temple. We must do what this book says. Call together all the people at the temple!

Narrator 2: The people sat and listened as the book was read to them. They were all sorry for the times they had disobeyed God and they promised to obey him in future.

Narrator 1: They had a special feast to show God they really meant what they said and, with Josiah's help, they read God's special book and did what it said.

Narrator 2: Four things happened to the book. First of all it was LOST (show flash card). Then everyone was so pleased when it was FOUND. The third thing that happened to it was that it was READ – read out to all the people so that they could listen to God's laws. Last of all the Book of Law was OBEYED.

Leader: Christians today still read God's special book to help them know how God would like them to live.

Follow up

Read the story of Mary Jones and how the Bible was so important to her.

Look at the different types of literature contained in the Bible (*ie history, poetry, law etc*). Find the longest and shortest books.

Talk about time capsules as a way of showing future generations how we live. What information would they put into a time capsule? Watch the video *Basil and the Big Battle* (produced by Scripture Union).

35 Bin Man and Robbish

Aim

For use in an 'environment week' to help the children to think about their responsibility to look after God's world.

Bible base

Genesis 1. The creation of the world.

Preparation

Discuss how they think the world began. Read Genesis 1. Give them a chance to make comments about it. Talk about verses 28b and 31. Do we look after the world in the way we should?

Paint a large picture of the earth. Then prepare plants, sun, moon, birds and fish which can be added to the picture during the assembly. Also paint things which can spoil our environment to be stuck on too.

Write poems about rubbish.

Looking round the classroom, list everything that has been taken from the environment to give us the things we use.

Make up some movement routines for Mars Bars wrappers, apple cores and empty crisp packets (see Bin Man and Robbish play for assembly).

Presentation

Reader: Genesis 1:10, 11, 14–18, 20–21, 24–25,
Others in the class add the various things onto the picture of the earth.

Reader: God told man to look after the fish, the animals, the birds on the earth and so man . . . (*here the different things that spoil our environment can be listed and added to the picture*).

Reader: I wonder if we are always very good at keeping the earth clean . . .

Bin Man and Robbish

(*Bin Man and Robbish enter tidying litter*)

N1: Who are you and how did you come to be tidying up?

B: It should be obvious. I'm Bin Man and he's Robbish and we have a long history of tidying up. In fact we go back to the Normans. My great grandad was Norman the litter collector, my grandad was Norman the road sweeper and my dad was Norman the dustman.

R: That sounds like our cue for a song.

(*Song from the rest of the class – My old man's a dustman*)

N2: It's important to have people like Bin Man and Robbish about because so many of us don't look after the world properly. Their continuous campaign has ensured a cleaner place for us to live in.

N1: Take for example this dustbin here. People have used it properly and put all their litter inside it.

N2: Ah yes, but have you seen down behind the dustbin . . .

(*Some of the children could read their poems on rubbish*)

N1: If we allow litter to build up we cause problems for ourselves.

N2: Sometimes these problems affect our health. You may have heard of the Great Plague of 1665 which was carried by rats. Imagine a modern day plague caused by litter.

(*Movement routines representing Mars Bars wrappers, apple cores and empty crisp packets.*)

R: Desperate dustbin liners, Bin Man!

B: Yes, you're right Robbish, that's what we need and lots of them! Luckily for us, here are some I made earlier. Now boys and girls all you need is some double-sided sticky tape and a plentiful supply of . . .

R: Er Bin Man, let's just concentrate on collecting the litter shall we?

B: Good thinking, Robbish. You start here and I'll start down behind the dustbin.

(*Bin Man and Robbish try to collect all the rubbish but the rubbish begins to close in on them.*)

R: Gee whizz, Bin Man, I get the distinct feeling that this rubbish is getting the better of us.

B: Keep calm, Robbish. I always keep a blow torch on me, just in case. We'll melt the Mars Bar wrappers!

(*The Mars Bars are melted away*)

N1: That was brilliant but how are they going to get rid of the other two plagues? Apple Cores and crisps don't melt.

N2: Perhaps they'll have to sweep them down behind the dustbin.

N1: But wait . . . what's this? Can it be that Bin Man has called in reinforcements?

(*Enter PB1 and PB2 on bikes*)

N1: Excuse me, who are you and what are you doing here?

PB1: We've come to help Uncle Bin Man.

N2: But why are you on bikes?

PB2: That's easy – we're Pedal Bin men.

(*They go over to the apples*)

PB1: You're rotten to the core.

AC: (*afraid*) Oh!

PB2: I don't find you appealing.

AC: Oh!

PB1: You give me the pip.

(*Apple cores go off mumbling and muttering*)

PB2: Ha, Ha we've made them stalk off

(*Ring bells and ride off*)

R: Golly gosh Bin Man, how did you know that one would work?

B: Well, Robbish, I'll never forget the day my mum taught me the secret of how to make an apple crumble.

R: We've got rid of two plagues, Bin Man, but I've never met a plague of crisps before.

B: I have a plan, but I'll need some help from the audience. When I count to three I want you to say 'boo' very loudly. Let's have a practice.

(*Practice and then real thing, crisps jump and then run out very scared*)

R: Peeling Potatoes! They seem pretty scared.

B: Yes, Robbish, I realised that underneath their hard exterior that they were really chicken crisps.

N1: Well, like all good stories this one has a happy ending.

N2: Bin Man and Robbish have cleared up all the rubbish. But what are you going to do to take care of the world that God has given us to look after?

Prayers thanking God for the world and asking for help to look after it.

An alternative to Bin Man and Robbish is to use Wesley Worm.

Wesley Worm

N1: What is it that you like about the earth most? Is it the rocks, sand, mud or dirt?

N2: I've got a friend who's greatest joy is *dirt* and his name is Wesley.

(*Enter Wesley, who is a worm!*)

N1: Hello, Wesley, how are you?

N2: Where have you been?

W: Playing hide and seek.

N2: Where have you been hiding? I haven't seen you.

W: That's because I'm good.

N1: So where have you been hiding?

W: In the soil, in the dirt.

N2: He says he is an earth worm.

N1: So what on earth do you do all day?

W: I dig holes.

N1: What!

(*N2 whispers in N1's ear*)

N1: What! He eats dirt!

N2: Yes, he eats it by the yard.

N1: Well, you'd better not come into my yard. So why do you eat dirt? What does that do?

W: Eating dirt keeps the ground clean.

N1: So you're like a hoover. Have you enjoyed eating the dirt?

W: Yes and . . . no.

N1: Why not?

W: My job is to keep the ground clean. When it is clean

135

then the plants can grow, because I dig holes and the air can keep clean. BUT there is a problem, a very big problem ... Cans! Cans, Cans, Cans!

N1: Why! What happens?

W: They make me sick, sick.

N2: But I thought you were meant to eat all the rubbish.

Pause

N1: Aren't you meant to look after the ground?

W: If I'm meant to look after what's in the ground, you have to be careful with what you put in the ground. No cans, or crisp packets. They are just awful. They aren't crisp at all, they go soggy, and so do sweet wrappers, they really get up my nose because there are so many of them! Why do people spoil the ground so I can't do my job properly?

N2: Because they don't think and don't remember.

W: You should try coming down and living in my place for a while. They shouldn't forget, because I've got a worm sized brain and they've got a bigger brain than me, so why don't they use it properly?

N1: OK I'll tell them.

An extra item for a Green assembly is to show the letters GREEN with the correct words folded up behind. Ask for suggestions of words beginning with that letter, before revealing the correct one. It stands for God's Riches Equal Everyone's Needs

Follow up

Look at ways they can improve the school environment.

Volunteer to keep a small area of school tidy.

Talk about things that they could recycle, organise a can collection etc.

Make a list of everything that is thrown out in your home for a day.

Prepare a one-minute presentation on an environmental problem.

Tackle each issue, encouraging the children to consider 'What can I do?'

Ask the children to recall being in a beautiful natural environment and allow them to express their feelings.

36   Sports Day

Aim

To look at the life of Eric Liddell and the example he set.

Preparation

Discuss with the children what they like most about Sports Day. Are there any children who don't like it? Could the children write about how it feels to win a race? Or to come last? Are there any other times when they feel the same way?

Talk about what we mean by 'He's a good sport' and 'She always puts herself in other people's shoes'

Which are their favourite athletes? Make fact-files on them. Do sportsmen and women always set us a good example? Do they ever let us down?

Is winning always the most important thing?

Read Hebrews 12:1–2, 1 Corinthians 9:24–26. Talk about why Paul compares living the Christian life to running a race.

Tell the story of Eric Liddell, the runner. Why did he give up his chance to win a gold medal?

Talk about times when they have felt like giving up. Have they ever thought they wouldn't learn something? Did they manage it in the end?

Presentation

Introduction: Play the theme music to Chariots of Fire.

Narrator 1: Some of us are keen on different sports: these children are going to tell you about their favourite sport and what is involved in it.

(*A few children talk about the sport they do, wearing the kit*)

Narrator 2: Many athletes put in a great deal of training so that they do well in their sport – it takes a lot of time and effort. Here we demonstrate how they might train for their favourite sports. (*Children can do press ups, running on the spot, handstands, balancing etc.*)

Narrator 3: If you are an Olympic athlete, the training is much harder and tougher. Often these athletes put in years of work for just one event. Here is a story about someone who was prepared to give up his chance of a gold medal because of what he believed in.

Reader: Eric Liddell was a sprinter who was picked to represent Britain in the 1924 Olympic games in Paris. He was very fast and was expected to win a gold medal in the 100 metres. However when he arrived he was sad to discover that the heats for the race were to be on a Sunday. Eric was a Christian and he believed Sunday was a special day to worship God. So he would not race. Many people tried to change his mind but he would not budge. Instead he entered the 400 metres, an event he hadn't trained for and nobody thought he had a chance. He won the gold medal. Just before this race he was handed a piece of paper. On it was a verse from the Bible which said 'I (God) will honour those who honour me.' (1 Samuel 2: 30).

Narrator 4: Eric stood up for what he believed in and didn't give up. There are lots of famous sportsmen and women who love Jesus even more than the sport which they enjoy.

Follow up

Contact Christians In Sport. Invite in a leading local sportsperson noted for his/her Christian response.

Write amusing stories about falls or mistakes in races – 'How I scrambled my egg in the egg-and-spoon race', 'cross legged in the three-legged race', etc.

37 The End of a Year . . .

Aim

To remind the children that change is a necessary part of life, and to help them to face new experiences.

Bible base

Malachi 3:6 and Ecclesiastes 3:1–8 God and Time. The Ecclesiastes passage reminds us that none of the circumstances around us remain unchanged for long, however much we wish they could, whilst the verse in Malachi reveals the unchanging nature of God.

Preparation

If there are children who are changing schools, give them a chance to express their hopes and fears for the future. Talk about any other fears they have for the future. They could write down what they think they would be doing in two, five, ten years' time. Ask if they can remember being frightened of something new ever before. How did they get over their fears?

Talk about the advantages of going to a new school: more subjects, new friends, more clubs (or whatever is applicable).

Discuss change in general terms. Think about all the different uses of the word 'change'. Look at the changes that happen regularly every year, or the changes in themselves as they grow up.

Write some 'change' poems; on the changing seasons, or the way their feelings change. Are these changes a good thing or not?

What would it be like if life went on the same for ever?

How would they like to change? How have they changed this year?

Look at characters in the Bible who changed eg. Zacchaeus, Paul, and Peter after Pentecost.

Mention some of the major changes that have taken place in the world, looking at the poem used in the assembly outline. Read the passage from Ecclesiastes with the children and prepare it for choral speaking.

Presentation

(There is a lot of material here for one assembly, so if preferred, use either the mimed drama or the choral speaking)

Leader: We are drawing near to the end of the school year and we are all facing some changes. Watch while these children show you a mime about change.

(Present the following as a mimed drama to narration)

When the world was younger than today,
Then man set out to hunt his prey,
With bow and arrow, spear and axe,
And eye to ground to follow tracks.
He chased the fierce and woolly beasts,
And turned their carcases into feasts,
Which fed the tribe for many days . . .
Until at last they changed their ways.

'The future lies in growing seed',
The wise man said, 'Now you take heed
Of these my words, and plough the soil,
Despite the backache and the toil.
Pull the plough behind the ox
And keep the fields full of your flocks.
You will be glad you changed your ways,
And sow and reap for all your days.'

Now Farmer Fred had sown his seeds
But found his fields so full of weeds.

His sons, called James and Sam and Ben,
Went out to pull them up again.
They took their barrows over there,
Their wheels, you won't believe, were square.
'It's hard to push it on this ground . . . (*not narrator*)
It might be better if they're round.'

The years passed by and out to play,
The young men came at close of day.
They loved to run and kick and fight,
Until the darkest shades of night.
The words they used were not cherubic,
The problem was the ball was cubic.
'We'll never win the Cup, I fear, (*not narrator*)
Unless we change it to a sphere.'

As man has gazed into the sky
He's envied creatures which can fly.
With feathers glued upon his arm,
He's never ceased to come to harm.
In fact no-one has yet been found
To lift themselves right off the ground.
'We'll stick to car and bike and train, (*not narrator*)
Until someone invents the plane.'

Now you may think that all this rhyme,
Is in the past, not in our time.
But there you might be very wrong,
For in September, not so long,
When you come back to school again,
After your hols in France and Spain,
You will find, now have no fear,
You have moved on another year.

Leader: All of us have nearly finished our time in one class
and after the holidays will be starting in a new class. For
some of us this is a special end; the end of our time in this
school before moving on to start a new school next term. (*It
is suggested that an appropriate song be sung here*).
   These children are going to recite a passage from the Bible

which talks about the different times there are in life.

Choral speaking:

Two solo voices and three groups of about four plus musicians playing drum, tambourine, cymbal etc.

(Drum beat)

Solo voice 1: There is a right time for everything. Everything on earth has its special season.

Solo voice 2: There is a time to be born

Group 2: and a time to die

Group 1: there is a time to plant and a time for pulling up

All: a time to kill *(strongly)*

Group 2: and a time to heal *(gently)*

All: There is a time to destroy and a time to build, to cry *(softer)* and to laugh *(louder, with a tambourine)*.

Solo voice 1: There is a time to be sad

All: and a time to dance *(tambourine)*

Group 3: A time to hug and not to hug. There is a time to look for something

Group 1: and a time to stop, a time to keep and to throw away.

All: A time for tearing

Group 2: and a time for sewing together.

Solo voice 1: A time to be silent *(stage whisper)*

(Pause)

Group 2: and a time to speak.

Groups 2 and 3: There is a time to love and the time for hate.

The time for war *(cymbal clash)*

Solo voice 2: And the time for peace.

Leader: For everything there is a time. For some of the people here their time in this school is nearly over. To all these people we have to say a special thank you for the way they have taken part in this school. Although we are all facing some changes the Bible says there is something that will never change – and that is God. (Read Malachi 3:6)

Follow up

None is included as it is not imagined you will have time for any!

Resources

Books for use in assembly
Assemblies for Primary Schools: M. Cooling (RMEP)
Ignatius goes fishing and *The reluctant Mole*: P. Welsh (SU)
Miles and the Computer and *Miles and the Church Outing*: T. Davies (SU)

Books for use in class and follow-up
Christianity Topic Books : M. Cooling (RMEP)
Faith in Action series (RMEP)
Feasting and Festivals (Lion)
How the Bible came to us: M. Doney (Lion)
How They Lived in Bible Times: G. Jones (SU)
How to be a church detective: (Falcon)
Jesus: The man who changed history: M. Doney (Lion)
Life in Bible Times (SU)
Life in the time of Jesus: M. Keene (Oliver and Boyd)
Living Festivals Omnibus (RMEP)
Look into the Bible (SU)
The Lion Christmas Book: M. Batchelor
The Lion Easter Book: M. Batchelor
The Christian World: A. Brown (Macdonald)

Scripture Union has produced a number of videos which could be used in lessons:
Basil and the Big Battle
David the Shepherd King
Exodus
Follow the Leader (stories from Matthew's Gospel)
Good Friday and Easter Sunday (Easter story)
Joseph

Luke Street (Stories from Luke's Gospel)
Mark Time (Stories from Mark's Gospel)
On Fire (Stories from Acts)
Shipshapes (Stories about the life of Peter)
Signposts (Stories from John's Gospel)

Videos are available from Scripture Union Bookshops, other Christian bookshops and suppliers or direct from Scripture Union Mail Order. Videos may also be hired from Scripture Union Mail Order, 9–11 Clothier Road, Bristol BS4 5RL. Tel 0272–719709. Fax 0272 711472.